תל אביב

TLV

JIGAL KRANT

Photography by Vincent van den Hoogen

CONTENTS

Join us: we're in the kitchen
talking about revolution.

Graffiti in Tel Aviv

The holy land is seen by many
as a gastronomic desert (...)
Its native cuisine is overshadowed by other,
more appealing international cuisines.

Capitool Travel Guide 2001

Israel, and Tel Aviv in particular, are
gastronomic destinations. The restuarant
culture is constantly in flux and reflects
Israelis' all-consuming love of food.

Capitool Travel Guide 2016

PREFACE

"Are we eating in a nightclub, or dancing in a restaurant?!" my friend asks, bewildered, as the rump of a mini-skirted beauty swings this way and that over his steaming lamb shawarma. This is his first encounter with the nightlife of Tel Aviv, where all forms of entertainment flow seamlessly into each other. We're sitting at the bar around the open kitchen of HaSalon, the flagship of Eyal Shani. The charismatic chef has several leading restaurants in the city, but on the two evenings that HaSalon is open, he can always be found behind the stove. As usual in Tel Aviv, that stove is not hidden in a fluorescent-lit kitchen, but is in full view of the guests. While Sephardic beats pump from the loudspeakers, and behind us two dancing boys lift a waitress up on a table, the chefs carry on, unperturbed. They're used to it. This is how it is every Wednesday and Thursday.

Nowhere is life celebrated more exuberantly than in Tel Aviv, the happiest and most tolerant city in the Middle East. This coastal city is paradise on earth, boasting great weather all year round, beautiful beaches, leading museums, unique architecture and a flourishing economy. The inhabitants are handsome, young, creative and radiate an unbridled zest for life. Nowhere can you eat better than in Tel Aviv. That rule applies first and foremost to the street, with its unsurpassed fast-food stalls serving hummus, falafel and sabich. In informal restaurants, the chefs put the rich eating traditions of Israel's immigrant population to good use. The result is an inventive culinary fusion without rules or taboos.

It has not always been this way. The Tel Aviv to which I lost my heart is nothing like the dreary eastern-block dump that I remember from 25 years ago. At the time, I lived just south of Jerusalem, but regularly came to Tel Aviv because I had fallen for someone who was studying there. The White City, barely sixty years old, was dilapidated. Little was left of its illustrious Bauhaus architecture. The population was restless and irritable, the level of prosperity low. To get a decent cup of coffee you had to leave the country. Apart from a handful of expensive restaurants, where unruly chefs frenetically imitated their French idols, food came mainly from snack bars and bleak cafeterias. The *kenjon*, the indoor shopping centre, was the highest form of entertainment. This culinary malaise affected the whole country, but nowhere was it more apparent than in Tel Aviv. I was always relieved when I arrived back in Jerusalem.

A quarter of a century later, the culinary elite can't stop talking about Tel Aviv. In world cities such as London, Paris, New York and Amsterdam, Israeli restaurants are sprouting like mushrooms. Star chefs are drawing inspiration from colleagues in Tel Aviv. Jerusalem is attracting more pilgrims than ever before: not devout Christians pushing a life-sized wooden cross on wheels along Via Dolorosa, but foodies on the lookout for the smells and flavours of their guru Yotam Ottolenghi.

Ottolenghi, born in Jerusalem, brought Israeli cuisine to an audience of millions with his cookbooks. Za'atar, harissa and orange-blossom water – products that nobody had heard of ten years ago – now take pride of place in the store cupboards of the contemporary hobby cook. Thanks to Ottolenghi, the attention of the Western culinary world has turned to Israel, but he was just a happy messenger with excellent timing.

A rare scene in Tel Aviv: ultra-orthodox Jews on the Rothschild Boulevard

At the end of the last century, Israel's turbulent society sailed into calmer waters. In 1993, the Intifada uprising died a silent death; and the last war dated from 1982. Along with peace came prosperity. A new generation of young people began reaping the rewards of the pioneering work their parents and grandparents had done and loosening the prevailing stays. Since the establishment of the state in 1948, there had been no time or money for decadent pursuits such as fashion, going out and culinary refinement. A new country had needed to be built up between the wars. By ostentatiously flirting with luxury and freedom, this third generation was rejecting what it saw as an oppressive society obsessed with war and religion.

At the same time, an increasingly significant dichotomy between the ultra-orthodox and secular population was taking place. The status quo could no longer resist the explosive growth of ultra-orthodoxy, the so-called Charedic community. Because of this community's excessively high fertility rate – an average of seven children per family – Jerusalem, always the Israeli city with the most Charedim, became steadily more devout. By the mid-1990s, for the first time in its history, the capital counted more orthodox than secular Jews. This demographic change had far-reaching consequences for public life. The level of prosperity dropped dramatically. Charedic men tend to fill their days studying religious texts. Unemployment is therefore above 50 percent. At the same time, ultra-orthodoxy was steadily imposing its religious will on the rest of the city's inhabitants. In 2000, the first bus route with segregated places for men (at the front) and women (at the back) started running. On Shabbat, entire districts became closed off to traffic. Those who turned down the wrong street on their bike ran the risk of being pulled off their saddle by enraged zealots. More and more neighbourhoods became no-go areas for fellow citizens who refused to follow the strictly imposed dress code. Advertising agencies applied self-censorship and removed stimulating images from their campaigns. Soon all images of women disappeared from the streets.

Due to the transformation of Jerusalem, secular Jews began to move to Tel Aviv en masse. The Charedic minority in Tel Aviv felt marginalised and moved to Jerusalem or the suburb of Bnei Brak. This is how the two largest cities of Israel became polarised: Tel Aviv secular and progressive, Jerusalem religious and right-wing nationalist. Nowadays, when I drive back into Tel Aviv after a day in Jerusalem, I instantly feel a weight being lifted from my shoulders.

The collision of all these factors – the relatively peaceful political climate, increased prosperity, the freedom reclaimed by the third generation and the ideological gap between Jerusalem and Tel Aviv – has given Tel Aviv a huge boost. As the city's nightlife rapidly expanded, so did the belief that freedom had to be exploited as best it could. Tel Aviv became a hedonistic city, a modern Sodom and Gomorrah in the eyes of the Charedim. Its restaurants served blatantly non-kosher food, with plenty of shellfish and crustaceans; kosher addresses, meanwhile, were few and far between. Since 2015, the arrival of many French Jews has changed that. The French immigrants, fleeing from increased anti-semitism in their homeland, are largely non-religious, but traditional.

The arrival of a number of decent kosher restaurants has not changed the identity of Tel Aviv's bustling hospitality industry – it remains plainly *treif* (non-kosher). Nowhere is this clearer than on the square around the Great Synagogue, where some of the city's most prominent restaurants have established themselves. In the shadow of the house of prayer, a monstrous structure in decline, religious food laws are trampled underfoot. The newest addition to Mount Sinai Square (the irony!) bears the name of a Christian saint: Santa Katarina. The snub to religious Judaism could not be more emphatic.

Another important development that has been crucial to the culinary revolution in Tel Aviv is the rehabilitation of Sephardic cuisine. For a long time the Sephardim, a collective term for Jews from Islamic countries, played a subordinate role in Israeli society. On a socio-economic, political and cultural level, the Ashkenazim (Jews of European origin) were dominant, and Sephardic food culture was viewed with disdain. Falafel was, admittedly, the nation's favourite dish, but this snack introduced by Yemeni and Iraqi Jews was consigned to the street. The same was true for pitta classics such as shawarma and sabich. Sephardic dishes that don't work as street food, such as shakshuka and chraime, could only be found in people's homes. Restaurants of any fame were built on the French model. However, by the end of the nineties, more and more chefs were beginning to realise that artful stacks of goose liver and truffle sauce just didn't cut it with Israelis. Instead of expensive imported products, they started to embrace local ingredients. Haute cuisine was exchanged for the cooking traditions of their grandparents. It proved a winning manoeuvre. Chic affairs disappeared from the streets and made way for informal restaurants where guests could eat in their flip flops. And dance. To Sephardic music.

The power of Tel Aviv's modern cuisine lies in its paradoxical combination of tradition and lack of tradition. On the one hand, Israeli society is a melting pot of cultures, each with its own rich culinary tradition – so in restaurants, where no two chefs have the same ethnic background, all those smells and tastes from Europe, North Africa and the Middle East flow together organically. On the other hand, Tel Aviv knows almost no restaurant tradition. Chefs do not have the shoulders of giants to stand on, but this also means they're not hindered by culinary taboos. Because of this, they feel free to innovate to their hearts' content.

Although still young and immature, modern Israeli cuisine can be defined by a number of distinctive features. In first place are its typical seasonings, such as tahini, za'atar, sumac and silan (see taste-makers, page 25).

A predilection for vegetables is also crucial. The chefs who contributed to this book all serve meat and fish in their restaurants, yet when I asked them to contribute a recipe to *TLV*, all came up with vegetable dishes.

In Israeli cuisine, the kitchen is simple and pure: it's the dishes, not the chefs, that are placed on a pedestal. Also key is the frequent use of naked flames. Eggplants (aubergines) and capsicums (bell peppers) charred over flames play a major role, and supposedly boring vegetables such as fennel, kohlrabi, sweet potatoes and beetroot (beets) are improbably flavourful after being grilled or baked in the fire for an hour or so.

In Israel, it's easy to eat out informally. Restaurants are accessible, noisy and not the exclusive domain of people over thirty.

Teenagers also go out for dinner together and then hang out all evening (and into the night). Many restaurants have a resident DJ and an extensive cocktail menu. Anywhere that serves food stays open until late at night and kitchens take orders right up to the last minute. Which is handy, because alcohol makes you hungry. That's why a typical evening out in Israel can both start and end with a meal (believe it or not, the photo on pages 162–63 was taken at 2am).

Eating in this country is a social event. Table-mates share their dishes, and to taste the food of a total stranger is very normal. The most popular spots in many restaurants are the stools at the bar surrounding the open kitchen. Here, the chefs are potential conversation partners and get in on the toast when the shot glasses are brought out. This happens more and more frequently as the evening progresses.

The most important ingredients in Israeli food are love and pleasure: both guests and staff demonstrate a greedy glee that's completely unique.

THE BUBBLE

This book is my culinary ode to my second home, which in many ways I know better than my home town of Amsterdam. As often as work and family commitments allow, I slip off to live the good life in Tel Aviv – especially since my parents have an apartment on Rothschild Boulevard, in the beating heart of the city. My parents are certainly not the only pensioners who have chosen to spend their twilight days with one foot in Tel Aviv. In all, tens of thousands of wealthy diaspora Jews have settled in Tel Aviv in recent years. As a result, house prices have risen exponentially. The Tel Aviv skyline is dominated by a growing number of residential towers and a multitude of construction cranes. The White City – so called because its centre is dominated by Bauhaus architecture – has visibly smartened up. National monuments have risen from the ashes; streets and parks are neatly tended.

The other side to this story is that the city has become unaffordable to the average Israeli. In 2018, property prices per square metre were more expensive in the centre of Tel Aviv than in the heart of New York or London. In the absence of rent protection, rental increases of tens of percent per year are the rule rather than the exception. Many of my friends have been forced to leave their beloved city. Young families have withdrawn to neighbourhoods such as Kiryat Ha'Melacha and Florentin, where they live in old sheds or workshops amid artists, metal workers, junkies and, of course, hipsters. Florentin has become a vibrant, multicultural neighbourhood, but project developers are lying in wait. Clandestine tattoo parlours have long since made way for bars serving triple-hopped IPAs or coffee tents doubling as

bicycle shops. All day long, groups on guided tours make the rounds of the graffiti artworks. The street art looks slicker by the day.

Latent anger over extremely high housing costs came to a head in 2011, when thousands of Israelis camped in tents on Rothschild Boulevard for weeks on end – right on the doorstep of what would become my parents' apartment. Among them were plumbers and doctors, artists and professors, garbage collectors and bankers. The government promised to intervene, but hasn't been able to turn the tide. And so Tel Aviv seems to have become a victim of its own success.

People always ask me why I don't live in Tel Aviv, considering that I find everything there so fantastic. Although there are really several reasons, I always respond with the same answer: because Tel Aviv is in Israel. No matter how progressive, tolerant and cheerful the city may be, the rest of the country is becoming more and more nationalistic, religious and intolerant. For good reasons, Tel Aviv is called 'The Bubble' by both its fans and its detractors. As the contrast between the city and the country becomes starker, that bubble threatens to burst. What particularly concerns me are the longstanding efforts of religious fundamentalists to bring the renegade Tel Aviv to heel. Already, 30 percent of the city's supermarkets are forced to close on Shabbat. It's only a matter of time before such pressure bursts the bubble.

This prediction is a rather sad way to conclude my introduction – but at least it gives us all the more reason to fully enjoy Tel Aviv while it's still the coolest city in the Middle East.

THE RECIPES

One-third of the more than one hundred recipes in *TLV* consists of interpretations of (modern) classics. Sometimes with a twist, such as in the red tabouleh (page 267), sometimes as authentic as possible, for example with the hummus (page 236). A dozen recipes were presents from my favourite chefs in Tel Aviv – the time I spent in their kitchens was so instructive and inspiring. I couldn't add all of their recipes to the book verbatim (for example because some ingredients are almost impossible to find outside of Israel) and I had to compromise a bit in terms of preparation – after all, the average home cook doesn't have a charcoal grill at their disposal. Despite the necessary concessions, I promise that these brilliant recipes will give you a true taste of Tel Aviv. The rest of the recipes, more than half of the book, are from my own imagination. They may have been cooked up in my kitchen in Amsterdam, but in spirit they are pure Tel Aviv.

Most of the restaurants mentioned in *TLV* are non-kosher, but the recipes *are* – that means no pork, shellfish or crustaceans, and no mixing of meat and dairy products (this means that the meat dishes are all suitable for people with lactose intolerance).

The chapters in *TLV* deal with different ways of eating. In 'Grab a Bite', finger food is the focus. Here you'll find classic and new pitta-based snacks, but also dishes that you wouldn't directly associate with street food. Cutlery is seen in Tel Aviv as a necessary evil, both in the kitchen and at the table. Whenever possible, even restaurant dishes are served without cutlery. For us Westerners this can take some getting used to (my father-in-law still eats the contents of his pitta with a knife and fork). I think eating with your hands is such an honest approach. Why would you distance yourself from such an intimate act?

'At the Table' features dishes to impress guests at leisurely lunches or dinner parties. This doesn't necessarily mean that you need to formally serve everyone. Put the pan on the table or serve the food in a large bowl, or even – as in many restaurants in Tel Aviv – on a piece of cardboard.

'Salatim' is the Israeli version of mezze or tapas. Salads feature here, of course, but in Israel, dipping sauces such as hummus and baba ghanoush also count as *salatim*. Nothing says 'party' better than a table laden with *salatim* – sharing is caring!

In the final chapter, 'Basic Recipes', I include recipes for flavours that crop up in this book time and again. I have listed these first in the ingredients section of each recipe so that you don't realise just before serving your dish that there's a whole extra sauce still to make.

Dear reader, it's time to open your heart and be seduced by the tastes and smells of sexy Tel Aviv. Or better yet: book a ticket to TLV and take this book as your culinary guide! If you have questions about the recipes or struggle to find certain ingredients, feel free to send me a message via Twitter or www.TLV-kookboek.nl.

TASTE-MAKERS

Winemakers who understand their trade will tell you that the quality of their wine is decided in the vineyard, not in the cellar. Even with the best will in the world, you can't make a top-flight wine from a bad harvest, however expensive your oak barrels may be. The same principle applies to cooking. In large part, success at the table is decided before you even start cooking: it depends on you buying quality produce at the market, the grocery store and – let's not pretend otherwise – the supermarket. That may sound logical, but the countless so-so dishes that I've reluctantly ploughed through at dinner parties can mostly be blamed on laissez-faire shopping.

Whereas with cooking (not baking, which is another story) you don't have to worry about whether or not to level a teaspoon, nonchalance when shopping is disastrous. During the writing of this book, I asked friends (in the social-media sense of the word) to test out recipes. It usually went well, but in about one-third of the cases, something went totally wrong. 'Quite tasty,' was one verdict, for example, 'but it all tasted a bit plain.' That's a shame, I told myself, but informative – after all, test-cooking is a learning exercise, not an ego trip. Only after some probing did I discover that the test tube in question had not been able to find minced lamb, so had substituted with beef. And oh yes, their very old oven had only been within one hundred degrees of the prescribed temperature when roasting the vegetables.

I learned a lot from this and similar feedback – unfortunately not so much about the quality of the recipes as about our pitiful grocery-shopping skills. Put simply, quality is key: with bad ingredients, even the best recipe can fail; with good ingredients, even the worst recipe can still enjoy some success. So go out there as a poacher-cum-detective-cum-casanova and seek out the very best produce. This sometimes means travelling an extra few kilometres or delving a little deeper into your wallet. At the dinner table, the extra effort and expense are repaid twofold. I'm afraid I can't help you find the fishmonger with the freshest bream or the greengrocer with the finest avocados. With the right attitude and a bit of trial and error, you'll be able to sort the wheat from the chaff. However, what I can give you is some advice about the main taste-makers in this book: make some space in your store cupboard.

TAHINI

Sesame seeds ground into a paste. Indispensable in hummus, baba ghanoush and halva. Mixed with lemon juice and water, it's the main sauce in Israeli cuisine. Both the pure sesame paste from the jar and the prepared sauce are called tahini. To avoid confusion in my recipes, I make a distinction between 'raw tahini' and the prepared sauce, which I simply call 'tahini'. Please never say 'tahini sauce'. It sounds just as redundant as 'pitta bread', 'mozzarella cheese' and 'tiramisu pudding'.

Raw tahini containing more than one ingredient is junk. However, raw tahini made with 100 percent sesame seeds doesn't necessarily guarantee quality, either. Quality is determined by the many processes required to transform sesame seeds into a smooth paste: before being crushed under a rotating millstone, the seeds are washed, peeled, dried and roasted. Besides, there are dozens of sesame varieties, all of which vary greatly in quality.

Separated raw tahini is not a good sign. The tahini at the bottom of the jar may be a little thicker than at the top, but a thick layer of oil under the lid does not bode well: buy this only in acute emergencies. Also avoid tahini from health-food stores. They were selling tahini long before anyone had ever heard of it, but sat on their laurels while other producers caught up and then surpassed them in quality.

The best raw tahini can be found in shops selling Israeli products or at corner shops specialising in Turkish or Moroccan goods, although there too you have to double-check whether the raw tahini actually consists of 100 percent sesame seeds (salt also counts as a surplus ingredient!). Furthermore, the country of origin gives a good indication of quality. As far as I'm concerned, the best brands are Palestinian, but Israeli and Lebanese tahini are also not to be sniffed at. A good choice is Al Arz from Nazareth, which is exported to many countries including the UK, Australia and the United States.

ZA'ATAR

Aromatic herb that grows in Israel, Palestine and parts of Syria. It's often translated as hyssop, oregano or thyme, but this is misleading. Za'atar is simply za'atar and certainly very different from the three herbs mentioned. Unlike most green herbs, za'atar is also worth bothering with in its dried form. Even more so, za'atar can instantly lift the average meal to a higher plane. Unfortunately, many jars of za'atar contain no discernible trace of za'atar. This isn't surprising, because its limited production can't keep pace with ever-growing demand. Confusingly enough, manufacturers also sometimes label the authentic herb as hyssop or (wild) thyme, but much can be deduced from the other ingredients. Dried za'atar is always mixed with other seasonings. If it's good, those seasonings will be sumac, sesame seeds and possibly a touch of olive oil. If the ingredient list is any longer, then the product is probably rubbish. To make choosing a good za'atar even more difficult, price has very little bearing on quality.

Even the expensive '100% pure' za'atar sold in some supermarkets and endorsed by celebrity chefs contains everything – thyme, marjoram, oregano, salt, basil – except za'atar. Israeli and Arab za'atar are often no better. In Middle Eastern neighbourhood supermarkets I've found the craziest ingredients name-checked on the labels: coriander, cumin, star anise, fennel, wheat, soy oil, citric acid, parsley, sunflower seeds, chilli powder and even – cross my heart and hope to die – coconut. Personally, I'm very fond of the za'atar from Nadia & Merijn's SOUQ range (nadiaenmerijnsouq. nl), especially the Palestinian variant, which has that delicious spicy, slightly musty aroma that's characteristic of true za'atar.

SILAN

Israeli date molasses. The biblical description of Israel as the 'land flowing with milk and honey' refers not to honey-bee honey, but to date honey. This syrupy extract is considered a typical Israeli product. Bearing in mind the biblical reference, this assumption is not entirely wrong – although the average Middle Eastern supermarket sells more or less the same stuff labelled as date syrup or molasses.

Always check the ingredients list before you buy: genuine silan is 100 percent pure date extract, but low-quality brands often dilute the date extract with cheaper sweeteners, water and E-numbers.

In recent years, silan has enjoyed growing popularity among vegans, who use it as a plant-based alternative to honey. I'm crazy about the rich taste of silan because hidden under all that sweetness lie bitter, sour and salt notes, too. The combination of silan and tahini is indescribably delicious. As long as I had pittas, tahini and silan, I could happily go it alone on a desert island.

SUMAC

Spice obtained by drying and grinding the berries of the the sumac tree. The deep-purple powder has a sour taste and is a zingy alternative to seasoning with freshly ground black pepper. As long as the manufacturer has kept far away from dyes and preservatives, the colour of your sumac gives a good indication of its freshness: the older the sumac, the browner it becomes.

BULGUR

In a supermarket in Tel Aviv, an employee gave me a strange look when I asked where the 'bulgur' wheat was. The Hebrew word has the same letters but in a different order – not only are the letters reversed, as always in Hebrew, 'ruglub', but also swapped around to make 'lugrub' ('burgul'). Three taboulehs later and I found myself back in an Israeli supermarket looking for 'bulgur' wheat. Determined not to go wrong again, I mentally racked up the letters in the right order while I searched for a shelf stacker, then asked, 'Where is the gulbur please?'

To prevent such confusion in your supermarket, I decided to use the Turkish term 'bulgur' in this book, which is the most common naming in English.

At first glance, bulgur resembles couscous, but the grains are coarser and have a nuttier flavour. In contrast to couscous, bulgur is pre-cooked at the factory and then ground.

To find the best bulgur, you're best off heading to a Middle Eastern supermarket. If you can find it, I recommend the excellent Turkish brand Duru. Note that the size of the grains varies from coarse to fine.

BALSAMICO

Italian vinegar, ideally made from cooked grape must. Good balsamic is syrupy, intensely aromatic and more expensive than grocery store imitations. Fortunately, you only need a little bit of it in any recipe. Traditionally, genuine balsamic vinegar is allowed to age and thicken for twelve years. That makes it absolutely delicious, but horrifyingly expensive. You pay the equivalent of 1 euro for one milliliter of that black gold.

Fortunately, there are enough very decent balsamics out there that have spent a little less time maturing in the barrel. For 250 ml (8½ fl oz/1 cup) of decent balsamic vinegar, you should still expect to pay about the same as for a mid-range bottle of wine in a restaurant. Alternatively, you could use that money to buy enough bog-standard supermarket balsamic to fill your bathtub. These cost so little because they're just caramel-flavoured wine vinegar.

Do yourself and your guests a great favour and buy a nice bottle of balsamic vinegar from an (Italian) delicatessen – or ask for one for your birthday. Used sparingly, it should last until your next birthday. And don't throw away your old balsamic vinegar – you'll need it for the recipes that require 'simple balsamic vinegar'.

POMEGRANATE MOLASSES

Syrup made from cooked pomegranate juice. The flavour is sweet, but also sour and a bit bitter. The syrup works well in dressings, marinades and sauces. Buy any sort of pomegranate molasses you can find. One may have more depth of flavour than another, but you can't really go wrong.

OLIVE OIL

After every trip to Tel Aviv, I land at Amsterdam's Schiphol Airport with about five litres of olive oil in my hand luggage. I always buy it in the duty free at Ben Gurion Airport, so that neither El Al Airlines nor security can object. Besides a touch of patriotism, there is a valid explanation for my desire to almost give myself a hernia hauling a product that's readily available at home all the way back from Israel: unlike the olive oil in our stores, Israeli olive oil mentions two key factors on its labels – the type of olive used and the degree of acidity.

For the dishes in this book I use oil from koroneiki or arbequina olives, with an acidity of 0.3 percent. Its mild, grassy aromas perfectly match the numerous vegetable dishes in Israeli cuisine. Sadly, this information is almost always missing from the bottles of Mediterranean olive oil that we can get our hands on. This means that making a well-considered purchase based on the label alone is difficult. It's a bit like trying to choose a good bottle of wine without knowing the grape variety or alcohol percentage – all you can do is keep tasting different olive oils until you find your favourite.

Anyway, the recipes in this book always use extra virgin olive oil unless the oil is being used to cook something. Expect to pay as much for a litre of good extra virgin olive oil as you would for a pricier bottle of wine from the supermarket. When it comes to baking and frying, opinions differ on whether or not it's worth using quality olive oil. Dutch cookbook author Yvette van Boven swears by extra virgin, while for Dutch food writer Sylvia Witteman, simple olive oil is good enough. On this issue, I'm with Witteman: therefore, in my recipes, I make a distinction between 'extra virgin' olive oil and 'simple' olive oil.

ROSEWATER AND ORANGE-BLOSSOM WATER

These add subtle flavours to Middle Eastern pastries, cocktails and desserts. Rosewater is distilled from rose blossoms; orange-blossom water from the blossoms of bitter oranges. At least, that's how it should be. In reality, most bottles – even those with impressive Arabic text on their labels – contain cheap chemical junk. Steer clear of these, unless you want your dessert to smell like like the glowing cheeks of Aunt Mildred at her eightieth birthday party.

Most rosewaters and orange-blossom waters are made and sold as bath products. Tasty blossom waters, such as those from Nadia & Merijn's SOUQ range (nadiaenmerijnsouq.nl), are over ten times more expensive than the chemically produced fakes. Fortunately, as with balsamic vinegar, you only ever need a little bit. And blossom waters keep for months in the kitchen cupboard.

HARISSA

Hot paste made from chillies, peppers, garlic and spices, originating from Tunisia and other North African countries. For use in sauces, stews, tagines and kebabs. Finally: a seasoning that is easy to source and costs little! Middle Eastern corner shops and some supermarkets sell harissa from the Tunisian city of Cap Bon, recognisable by the lighthouse on its label.

EAT WITH YOUR HANDS

Miznon

THE THIRD PITTA SNACK

Almost everyone knows that you can find a pitta filled with falafel or shawarma on every street corner in Israel. However, there is a third pitta filling that's virtually unknown outside the borders of the Holy Land.

This improbably tasty vegetarian bite is called sabich, and it threatens to dethrone falafel as the nation's most popular street food. I don't have statistics, but you only have to take a look at the intersection of Frishman and Dizengoff to get the picture. Here, a street-food vendor operates two unsightly snack bars: Falafel Frishman on the left, and Sabich Frishman on the right. When hunger strikes, you're better off heading left, because the queue on the right is always long. This is something the owner didn't anticipate when he started his double enterprise years ago. Otherwise, he wouldn't have allowed one employee to be working his fingers to the bone making sabich pittas in a glorified walk-in closet while his falafel colleague is cooling his heels in plenty of space..

Since everything tastes better after you've spent fifteen minutes queueing for it with *savlanut* ('patience'), you join the back of the right-hand queue. When you get to the front, the sabich seller will ask you curtly: *hakol?* ('everything?'). If you answer in the affirmative – and you will, because with hungry Israelis breathing down your neck in the queue behind you, it's best not to get fussy – then a little miracle occurs. The seller cuts open your pitta with a stanley knife and stuffs it fuller than you ever thought possible with deep-fried eggplant (aubergine), a green sauce, a yellow sauce, a thick grey sauce, a thin white sauce, hard-boiled egg, cottage cheese, fries, red-onion rings, parsley and a variety of salads. Give it a try.

Enjoying an everything-sabich is anything but a chore, but the true purist would opt for only crisp-fried eggplants, a simple salad of tomato and cucumber, egg and four sauces in his sabich. In addition to tahini and a lick of hummus, the sauces are zhug (a hot-pepper sauce) and amba (a kind of spicy mango chutney).

Nobody knows for certain, but the word 'sabich' probably derives from the Arabic word for 'morning'. Traditionally it was eaten by Iraqi Jews for breakfast on Shabbat. Since cooking on Shabbat is forbidden, people fried the eggplants the day before and ate the sabich cold as a salad, without pitta.

After their emigration to Israel, many Iraqi Jews settled in Ramat Gan, a city cut off from Tel Aviv by the highway. It was in Ramat Gan during the 1950s that sabich developed into an everyday street food. Thereafter, the eggplant strips were fried to order until crisp on the outside and deliciously tender on the inside – and like all Israeli street food, the snack ended up in a pitta. Sabich has become increasingly popular in recent years, especially among young people. They see the snack as a healthy and hip alternative to shawarma and the somewhat old-fashioned falafel, the favourite of their parents and grandparents.

6 Sephardic brown eggs (page 303)
   or hard-boiled eggs
3 × quantities tahini (page 282)
3 × quantities quick Israeli salad (page 291)
1 × quantity amba (page 307)
1 × quantity zhug (page 306)

6 firm eggplants (aubergines)
sea salt flakes
sunflower or peanut oil for frying
12 large pittas

Prepare the Sephardic brown eggs, sauces and salad. If already prepared, remove from the fridge to bring them up to room temperature. Before peeling the eggs, soak them in hot water.

Peel narrow strips from the skin of the eggplants all down their length (by doing so you will avoid dragging all of the eggplant filling out of your sabich with the first bite). Cut into finger-thick slices and sprinkle all over with coarse sea salt. Set aside until beads of moisture can be seen on the surface of the eggplants. Shake off any excess salt and pat dry with paper towel.

Heat the oil in a deep-fat fryer or heavy-based frying pan to 180°C (350°F). Fry the eggplant slices in the hot oil, in batches if necessary, until dark brown on both sides but not crisp. Drain on a plate lined with paper towel and keep warm.

Toast the pittas and cut them open (watch out for the steam escaping). Spread the insides with tahini then fill with the salad, eggplant and crumbled egg. Finish with another tablespoon of tahini, two teaspoons of amba and a teaspoon of zhug. Serve in napkins with a cold beer – and plenty more napkins, toilet paper or kitchen paper.

SABICH

Just as the average Japanese home cook would never think to make sushi from scratch, few Israelis ever make sabich at home. Why would they? There's a stall on every street corner where for next to nothing you can get a warm pitta filled with crunchy eggplant (aubergine), egg, a quartet of salads and half a dozen sauces. And because it's easy to lose half a day to making sabich, what with shopping for groceries and preparing the various components, Israelis prefer to trust their sabich to the experts.

For anyone who doesn't live in Israel, it's a little more complicated. After that first unforgettable sabich experience you can't wait for your next trip to Tel Aviv. Meanwhile, back at home (at least in the Netherlands – until a canny entrepreneur fills this particular gap in the market) you can only find pittas stuffed with falafel and shawarma. So there's nothing for it but to roll up your sleeves and make it yourself.

Sabich is particularly good if you've invited a large group of people round, for example to celebrate a birthday or watch the football – activities which, for inexplicable reasons, seem to make everyone terribly hungry, but which preclude normal table manners. With enough preparation, the only last-minute things you need to do are to slide the eggplant into the fat and put the pittas in the toaster. It's win-win: you don't miss out on the action and you save yourself a lot of washing up. Another advantage of making sabich for a group is that it's suitable for all kinds of dietary requirements: it's kosher, halal, vegetarian, lactose free, nut free, pacifist and homeopathic. For vegans, simply leave out the hard-boiled egg. There are always one or two party poopers with a supposed gluten intolerance; you should resolutely show these people the door so as not to dampen the party vibes. In the unlikely event that you have to cater for a true coeliac, scrap the pitta, then arrange all the other ingredients artfully on a plate and call it a 'deconstructed sabich'.

LAMB SHAWARMA
IN LAFFA

Serves 4

1 × quantity laffa (page 300) or other
   unleavened bread
1 × quantity tahini (page 282)
1 tablespoon TLV spice mix (page 288)
   or ras el hanout/baharat

600 g (1 lb 5 oz) boneless leg of lamb, cut
   into 7.5 cm × 2.5 cm (3 in x 1 in) pieces
1 tablespoon za'atar
2 tablespoons wine vinegar
extra virgin olive oil
juice of ½ lemon, plus extra to season
3 vine tomatoes, diced
1 small red onion, chopped
2 Lebanese (short) cucumbers, diced
2 gherkins, cut into thin strips
6 oregano sprigs, chopped
4 flat-leaf (Italian) parsley sprigs, chopped
salt and freshly ground black pepper

Shawarma derives its name from the vertical rotating spit on which the spicy meat is roasted: this Arabic name comes from the Turkish *çevirme* ('turning'). Not many of us have a spit at home – but the same goes for most restaurants in Tel Aviv, which nevertheless serve dishes called shawarma on the menu.

Then they're not really serving shawarma, I remarked to top chef Eyal Shani, when I was preparing lamb shawarma under his supervision in the kitchen of his restaurant, Tzfon Abraxas (North Abraxas). According to the inimitable Shani, I was seeing it from the wrong angle. In his parallel universe, shawarma is not a cooking method, but a philosophy – one that can just as easily be applied to fish or vegetables. A little later, a sous chef whispered to me that what this philosophy actually comes down to is the idea of 'thin slices'. So forget the spit and sharpen your kitchen knife.

Massage the lamb with the za'atar and the spice mix. Add the wine vinegar, a generous splash of olive oil and the lemon juice, then mix well, cover and leave in the refrigerator to marinate – the longer the better.

Drain the diced tomato in a fine-mesh sieve, then mix it with the onion, cucumbers, gherkins and herbs. Season to taste with salt and freshly ground black pepper, and a little more lemon juice and olive oil.

Preheat the oven to 180°C (350°F). Heat a heavy-based frying pan over high heat. Remove the lamb pieces from the marinade and chargrill in batches for 1–2 minutes on both sides. Transer to the oven for 5 minutes, then slice into thin strips.

Spread each laffa with tahini and spoon the salad and lamb into the centre. Fold the bottom edge of each laffa over the filling so that the contents can't fall out, then roll them up from left to right. Wrap in a napkin (or, to be truly authentic, a sheet of newspaper) and serve immediately.

ARAYES

1 × quantity tahini (page 282)

1 tablespoon TLV spice mix (page 288)
or ras el hanout/baharat

2 tablespoons pine nuts

500 g (1 lb 2 oz) minced (ground) lamb or
mutton (minimum 15–20% fat content)

1 red onion, finely chopped

2 garlic cloves, crushed or finely chopped

1 teaspoon harissa

3 tablespoons finely chopped flat-leaf
(Italian) parsley

salt and freshly ground black pepper

4 pittas

extra virgin olive oil

2 ripe tomatoes, finely chopped or grated

1 Lebanese (short) cucumber, finely
chopped or grated

1 teaspoon lemon juice

Thanks to their smooth, crisp exterior and soft inner side, pittas lend themselves perfectly to toasted sandwiches (toasties). Moreover, with pittas you don't have to worry about the filling splurting out from all sides. Toasted sandwiches filled with spicy minced lamb are called *arayes*. Chef Jonathan Borowitz of meat-centric restaurant M25 claims to have introduced this Lebanese dish to Tel Aviv. Whether it's true or not, *arayes* have quickly become one of the most popular snacks in the city. This is my version.

The success of this simple dish stands or falls on the fat content of the minced meat. It should be 15–20 percent; discuss this with your butcher. Mutton is fattier than lamb, but the strong flavour of mutton is not for everyone. More fat means more flavour and makes the filling smoother. It also ensures that the meat filling melts, as it were, into the pitta. If you can only find lean minced meat, add 1 tablespoon of schmaltz (page 308) or other fat to the mixture.

Dry-fry the pine nuts until golden-brown, shaking the pan regularly and watching carefully so that they do not burn. Chop them coarsely, then knead them into the minced meat together with the onion, garlic, harissa, TLV spice and parsley. Season with salt and freshly ground black pepper.

Preheat the oven to 180°C (350°F).

Cut the pittas across the middle to create two half-moon-shaped pockets. Divide the filling mixture equally among the 8 pitta halves (about 75 g/2¾ oz per serving). Heat a chargrill pan over high heat. Brush the outsides of the pittas with oil, then sear the cut sides for 1 minute. Grill the pittas for 4–5 minutes on each side, until they are golden brown all over and striped with chargrill marks.

Transfer the arayes to the oven for 3–5 minutes, until the filling is cooked through.

Meanwhile, mix together the tomatoes and cucumber and season to taste with the lemon juice, extra virgin olive oil, salt and freshly ground black pepper.

Cut the arayes into quarters and serve with a bowl of tahini topped with the salad.

Arayes in Ha'achim

STREET SANDWICHES

Although you also come across them in restaurants, and every household keeps emergency rations in the freezer, the pitta is above all the sandwich of the street. Anyone wanting to assess the importance of the pitta to Israeli cuisine should first and foremost get acquainted with the streets of Israel. With a bit of imagination you can conjure up those streets, the local traffic a chaos of blaring horns and dented white Japanese-made cars driven by temperamental hotheads. But whereas for us, public roads are a handy piece of infrastructure to help us travel from A to B, for Israelis the street is an extension of the living room – and often a destination in itself.

Certainly, staying outside is preferable to sweltering inside during Tel Aviv's long, stifling summers. And the fact that, due to exorbitant house prices, most apartments are so petite that you and I would get claustrophobic after just one night, makes spending as much time as possible in the open air the only sane choice. The city is set up accordingly. Busy traffic arteries have leafy green strips down the middle, where the mood is reminiscent of Amsterdam's canal-side terraces on the first warm spring day of the year (only day in, day out).

Israelis experience their streets in a unique way: just take a seat on one of the many benches and you'll see young parents changing their baby's nappy, students prepping for their exams and couples demonstrating their love. Young and old alike perfect the art of doing nothing without anyone taking umbrage. The police have never heard of the phenomenon of loitering. Above all, the streets are one big open-air restaurant. Wherever you are in the city, you're only ever a stone's throw from all sorts of stalls selling all sorts of snacks. With the pitta as a common denominator.

The pitta is also a damn good invention: a sandwich that also serves as a plate. Shame they're inedible, you're thinking – but that's because you're used to the cardboard supermarket versions sold outside of Israel. Believe me: real, freshly baked pittas are the best bread you'll ever taste – smooth on the outside and fluffy and soft inside – so it's worth dedicating some time to finding the best pittas in your area. Start your search in the nearest multicultural neighbourhood: the pittas from a random Middle Eastern bakery will already taste miles better than the supermarket ones.

PITTA WITH LAMB MEATBALLS

After dropping off the children at school, I cycle straight to Amsterdam's Centraal station. If I catch the train in time, then by noon I'll be stepping onto the platform of Gare du Nord, in Paris with just enough time for a two-hour lunch at Miznon, in the 4th arrondissement. This Miznon is a branch of the famous Tel Aviv pitta restaurant, owned by my favourite Israeli chef Eyal Shani. I have drawn up a tight schedule. According to my calculations, if I write the restaurant review for my weekly food column on the train home, I'll meet my deadline and arrive on time to pick up my kids from their after-school activities. Call me childish, but I'm already giggling at the prospect of getting home and chuckling that nobody knows I had lunch in Paris.

It's a dreary Monday afternoon, but when I step into Miznon it's packed. Although Le Marais is home to dozens of falafel bars, all full of tourists trying to recapture the long-ago flavours and atmosphere of the Jewish quarter, there are only locals in Miznon. A rousing mixure of Israeli and French music blares from the speakers. Tightly packed customers queue up along the counter to place their order, which is prepared before their eyes.

I manage to find a seat by the window – whose sill, like every other empty surface in the place, is laden with cauliflowers, tomatoes and broccoli. From here, I can observe the whole happy cacophony. I don't need to stand in line, because manager David has granted me VIP status and insists on bringing everything to me. The menu is no carbon copy of the original restaurant in Tel Aviv. The French operators have given an Israeli twist to Gallic classics such as boeuf bourguignon and chou farci. Everything is served in a pitta; everything is delicious. They don't do falafel and shawarma here – for that you need to go to one of the neighbours.

Stomach full, I hurry back along Rue Saint-Martin to the station. On the train I call my local kosher deli and ask them to save me half a kilo (about a pound) of minced (ground) lamb. I file my review just as the train is pulling into Amsterdam Centraal ('worth a day trip to Paris for the pitta with lamb meatballs alone'). I collect my offspring and get to the deli just before closing time. 'Nice', my wife says that evening, sinking her teeth into a pitta with lamb meatballs. 'Your own recipe?'

Serves 5

1 × quantity tahini (page 282)
1 × quanity zhug (optional; page 306)
1 tablespoon TLV spice mix (page 288)
   or ras el hanout/baharat

handful of pine nuts
500 g (1 lb 2 oz) minced lamb
1 small red onion, finely grated
2 garlic cloves, crushed
1 teaspoon harissa
5 flat-leaf (Italian) parsley sprigs, coarsely
   chopped
salt
4 large vine tomatoes, thickly sliced
4 large onions, peeled and thickly sliced
extra virgin olive oil
sea salt flakes
5 pittas
4 coriander (cilantro) sprigs, leaves coarsely
   chopped

Preheat the oven to its hottest grill (broiler) setting (preferably 300°C/570°F without fan assistance). Spread the pine nuts on a baking tray and grill for 1 minute, or until lightly golden. Watch carefully and shake the tray regularly as they will burn easily. Chop coarsely.

Mix the pine nuts, lamb, red onion, garlic, harissa, TLV spice, parsley and a good pinch of salt. Shape the mixture into balls the size of falafel.

Arrange the tomato and onion slices in separate oven dishes. Drizzle with olive oil and season with sea salt flakes. Grill, turning once, until tender and caramelised on both sides – about 10–25 minutes (a few minutes extra for the tomatoes).

Fry the meatballs in oil for 4–5 minutes, until golden brown on both sides and cooked through. Toast the pittas until hot but not crisp. Cut them open and spread the insides generously with tahini, then fill with the meatballs, onion and tomato. Finish each with an extra drizzle of tahini and a sprinkling of coriander leaves. To spice things up, add a drizzle of zhug.

MIZNON'S MINUTE STEAK PITTA

Long before anyone had heard of fancy fast food, top chef Eyal Shani opened a snack bar in Tel Aviv. The charismatic celebrity chef was a man on a mission: the pitta, seen by Israelis as the most banal of all foodstuffs, needed a makeover. In a no-frills dining room, Shani served pittas filled with signature dishes from his renowned restaurants: I mean, why serve sirloin steak or chicken livers on cold plates when you can slide them into velvety, steaming pittas? The sophisticated palates of hip Tel Aviv were instant converts, and all at once the pitta was deemed beyond cool. As a food writer for the *Financial Times* so aptly put it: what George Clooney did for grey hair, Eyal Shani did for the pitta.

Coincidence or not, after Shani put pittas back on the map, Michelin-starred chefs around the world took a new look at humble folk food. In the Netherlands, Robert Kranenborg flipped burgers, Ron Blaauw fried hotdogs and Sergio Herman opened a chip shop. But in my view they all made the same error of judgement: they thought their street food 2.0 should be a chic and stylish affair with 'atelier' or 'boutique' in its name. It was expensive, because it was 'junk food' with a lick of truffle mayonnaise, a slice of goose liver or a garnish of duck-skin croûtons. If this was street food, it was from a street like Rodeo Drive.

Eyal Shani's approach was completely different. He called his restaurant Miznon ('snack bar' in Hebrew), and in keeping with the average snack bar, it looked a bit shabby. The sauce pumps dispensed not béarnaise or truffle mayonnaise, but good old tahini. Miznon just served a quick bite. It was high on quality, low on attitude.

This successful formula got a lot of attention outside Israel. Miznon swiftly grew into a global fast-food chain with franchises in Vienna, Paris, New York and Melbourne. I can't wait for someone to bring Miznon to Amsterdam! Until a branch opens up near you, this recipe – which I copied from the original Miznon on the corner of Ibn Gabirol and Dizengoff – should keep you sweet.

Serves 4

1 × quantity tahini (page 282)

4 × 100 g (3½ oz) minute steaks, cut against the grain, at room temperature
extra virgin olive oil
3 vine tomatoes, thinly sliced
1 green chilli, thinly sliced into rings
1 Lebanese (short) cucumber, cut into long, thin strips
1 gherkin pickle, cut into long, thin strips
1 spring onion (scallion), coarsely chopped
2 coriander (cilantro) sprigs, leaves chopped
2 flat-leaf (Italian) parsley sprigs, chopped
1 tablespoon lemon juice
sea salt flakes and freshly ground black pepper
4 pittas

To get your steaks as thin as possible, sandwich them between plastic wrap and flatten out with a meat mallet. Rub with a little olive oil.

Mix the tomatoes, chilli, cucumber, gherkin, spring onion and herbs together, and season with a drizzle of olive oil, the lemon juice, sea salt flakes and freshly ground black pepper.

Heat a chargrill pan until piping hot. Grill the steaks for 20 seconds on one side, then flip over and grill for a further 10 seconds. Sprinkle the meat with a little sea salt and set aside to rest.

Warm the pittas in a toaster. Cut each pitta open, spread the insides with tahini, then fill with the salad and the 'minute steak'.

Serves 6

2 tablespoons white sesame seeds

2 tablespoons black sesame seeds

2 teaspoons za'atar

1 teaspoon cayenne pepper

1 teaspoon sumac

sea salt flakes and freshly ground black
    pepper

600 g (1 lb 5 oz) fresh tuna fillet

12 rosemary sprigs

extra virgin olive oil

1 tablespoon balsamic vinegar

2 tablespoons toasted pine nuts

Dry-fry the white and black sesame seeds over medium heat, shaking the pan until the white seeds turn pale brown. Keep an eye on the seeds as they will burn quickly. Tip the seeds into a bowl with the za'atar, cayenne pepper, sumac and a pinch of sea salt flakes.

Dice the tuna into 3 cm (1½ in) cubes. Press two sides of each cube into the spice mixture. Pierce the cubes of tuna all the way through with a skewer or knitting needle, then thread two or three cubes onto each rosemary sprig.

Brush the tuna with olive oil. Heat a chargrill pan over high heat until very hot (this will take a few minutes). Grill the skewers on all sides until the tuna has golden-brown chargrill stripes on the outside but is still raw inside.

Pile the tuna skewers on a platter or divide them among individual plates. Drizzle with a little extra virgin olive oil and a few drops of syrupy balsamic vinegar. Season with lots of freshly ground black pepper and sprinkle with the pine nuts.

TUNA ON ROSEMARY SKEWERS

For a country with a coastline of almost 300 kilometres, Israel has a weak fishing culture. The first generations of Israelis hailed mainly from countries without a sea border. They only knew a few traditional freshwater-fish dishes, such as the notorious gefilte fish (page 170). In 1948, the year of Israeli independence, the national fishing fleet consisted of just four rickety ships. Not until the end of the last century did Israel start to become a fish-loving country. In the restaurants of coastal cities, with Tel Aviv leading the way, fish gradually appeared on more and more menus. The fishing industry grew explosively and uncontrollably, with the unfortunate result that fish numbers rapidly nosedived. Commercial fishing in the Gulf of Eilat was forced to stop after the last tuna was hoisted out of the water. The current conditions in the eastern Mediterranean are not much better. At the daily fish auction in Jaffa the fish are smaller in number and size with every passing year.

This is not very noticeable in food markets and restaurants in Tel Aviv: consumption continues to rise unhindered. What local fishermen can't catch themselves is just imported. It's as if Israelis, after decades of ignoring fish, are making up for lost time. Raw preparations such as sashimi, carpaccio, tartare and ceviche are especially popular with young Israeli chefs.

The success of this photogenic dish made with rare-cooked tuna depends entirely on the freshness of your fish. Ask a fishmonger whom you trust for sushi-grade tuna, and check its sustainability – overfishing is not an exclusively Israeli problem, and some tuna species are threatened with extinction worldwide. Fortunately, there are also species whose stocks are more buoyant and which may safely be eaten again. In any case, save this dish for special occasions.

PRONOUNCED FLAVOURS

'I'd rather starve than eat that shawarma! You have to go to Bino on the corner of Rothschild and Maze.'

An old joke tells of how a shipwrecked Jewish man is washed up on an uninhabited island. After many lonely years, a passing ship notices his smoke signals. Before the Jew climbs aboard, he shows the captain around his island: the hut where he lived, the synagogue where he prayed and the country house where he spent his holidays. At the end of the island tour, the captain catches sight of another building that the Jew has ignored. Reluctantly, the Jew tells him that this, too, is a synagogue. 'So you already had a house of prayer on the island?' the captain asks in amazement. 'Yes,' answers the Jew, 'but you don't think I'd ever set foot in that place, do you?'

Synagogues play a marginal role in secular Tel Aviv, but ask a random group of people where to find the best shawarma in the city and you'll witness a discussion swiftly escalating into an argument. 'Definitely HaKosem!' one will cry. 'Don't listen to him,' says a second, throwing up his hands. 'You have to go to Torek Lahmajun.' A third shakes his head violently, aghast at so much shamelessly displayed ignorance. 'I'd rather starve than eat their shawarma! You have to go to Bino on the corner of Rothschild and Maze.' And me? I think homemade shawarma are the most delicious.

CHICKEN SHAWARMA PITTA

Serves 4

1 × quantity tahini (page 282)
1 × quantity quick Israeli salad (page 291)
1 × quantity zhug (optional; page 306)
1 tablespoon TLV spice mix (page 288)
    or ras el hanout/baharat
1 tablespoon schmaltz (page 308)
    or olive oil

2 teaspoons ground cumin
2 teaspoons pomegranate molasses
1 teaspoon harissa
extra virgin olive oil
salt and freshly ground black pepper
600 g (1 lb 5 oz) chicken thigh fillets,
    cut into thin strips
2 onions, finely grated
2 garlic cloves, finely chopped
4 pittas

The meat rotating on the spit in Israeli restaurants is usually chicken or turkey, often enriched with lamb fat. Of course, lamb makes the tastiest shawarma, but lamb meat is more expensive and much more harmful to the environment. Save it for special occasions – see the recipe for lamb shawarma in laffa on page 43.

Shawarma made with chicken is less flavourful, but on the plus side, the meat is more tender and easier to digest than lamb. Always go for thigh meat: it's juicier, fattier and cheaper than overrated chicken breast.

Mix the spices, pomegranate molasses, harissa and a generous splash of olive oil in a bowl and season with salt and freshly ground black pepper. Add the chicken strips and stir to coat. Marinate in the refrigerator for at least one hour.

Heat the schmaltz in a frying pan over low heat. Fry the onions and garlic for 8–10 minutes, until softened. Increase the heat, shake the excess marinade from the chicken and fry for 3–5 minutes, until cooked through.

Warm the pittas in a toaster, then cut them open and smear the inside of each with tahini. Fill each pitta with chicken shawarma and salad, and finish with a generous extra drizzle of tahini – plus a little zhug, if desired, for sharpness.

Serves 5

500 ml (17 fl oz/2 cups) full-cream
  (whole) milk
125 ml (4 fl oz/½ cup) whipping cream
1 tablespoon rosewater
50 g (1¾ oz/¼ cup) sugar
35 g (1¼ oz/¼ cup) cornflour (cornstarch)
5 pinches of ground cinnamon
35 g (1¼ oz/¼ cup) roasted pistachios,
  roughly chopped

Whisk the milk, cream, rosewater,
sugar and cornflour in a saucepan until
no lumps remain. Place the pan over
medium heat and bring the mixture to
the boil, stirring all the time.

Reduce the heat as soon as the mixture
begins to thicken. Stir for another
1 minute, then turn off the heat.

Pour the hot sachlab into five small
heatproof glasses and sprinkle with
the cinnamon and chopped pistachios.
Serve immediately.

SACHLAB

Everything is relative, my grandmother used to say. I think of her every winter in Tel Aviv. Because if that wise old saying applies to anything, it applies to the Israeli winter. The Israelis have a word for winter: *horef.* Then again they also have a word for peace (*shalom*), so that doesn't mean much.

For their annual dose of winter fun, Israelis must travel to Mount Hermon, a mountain in the far north. You can ski there, but don't get too excited: the 2814-metre high mountain can't hold a candle to Aspen or the Alps.

In the high-lying city of Jerusalem, a sporadic flurry of snow will sometimes fall. All photographers then rush to the Wailing Wall to take fairytale-like pictures. These shots are so popular with makers of calendars and postcards that anyone browsing the country's souvenir shops would be forgiven for thinking that Israel's winters are akin to those in Siberia.

In Tel Aviv, about 60 kilometres from Jerusalem, a winter's day is only slightly more inclement than the average summer's day. But because everything is relative, and because in Tel Aviv the average temperature difference between summer and winter is about 20°C (68°F), you'll find the inhabitants dressing as if for a polar expedition when in fact it's 15°C (59°F) outside. At the beginning of January my children, with their sleeveless shirts, look as if they don't belong in the same Israeli playground as their peers, who are dressed head to toe in three thick layers of down.

At the Carmel Market in winter, almost every market vendor goes about his business clad in thermal socks, mittens and ear muffs. In order to put paid to the phantom cold, an Israeli Arab pours scalding hot *sachlab* from an Aladdin-like copper kettle. *Sachlab* is the Israeli counterpart to our hot chocolate: a sweet drink made with milk and cream, delicately perfumed with rosewater, then topped with chopped nuts and cinnamon. This treat comes from Turkey, where real winters actually do exist. Turkish *salep* is thickened with a powder made from dried, ground orchid tubers. In Israel, cornflour (cornstarch) is used instead. It works equally well, but it means the name of the drink is no longer accurate – 'salep' and 'sachlab' mean 'orchid' in both languages.

On the other hand, I thought, in clever-clogs mode, hidden in the word 'sachlab' (סחלב) is 'chalav' (חלב), the Hebrew word for milk. The same cannot be said of the Turkish *salep* ('milk' is *süt* in Turkish). When you then, as with a Russian doll, remove another layer, you find that the word 'chalav' contains 'lev' (לב), the Hebrew word for heart. That's my warm-and-fuzzy interpretation – I'll leave you to come up with your own.

By the way, *sachlab* vendors disappear from the streets like snow in the sunshine when spring comes to Tel Aviv, usually in mid-February. But don't worry if you're only in Tel Aviv in summer – the solid version of this drink, *malabi*, is available all year round and is just as delicious (see page 213). We make *sachlab* at home in Amsterdam during the winter months. Because even though our winters are getting milder every year, they're still ferocious compared with those of Tel Aviv.
As Grandma used to say: everything is relative.

ISRAEL'S NATIONAL SNACK

The consensus among culinary historians is that fried chickpea balls originated in Egypt at least a thousand years ago. Yet still there are Israeli patriots who argue wide-eyed that falafel is a Jewish invention.

For as long as I can remember, Israeli souvenir shops have sold a postcard with a photo of a pitta filled with falafel on the front. The accompanying text reads: 'Falafel – Israel's national snack'. Plunged into one of the falafel balls, at an iconic angle reminiscent of American soldiers raising the flag on Iwo Jima, is a tiny paper Israeli flag on a cocktail stick. That analogy is proof for many that Israel stole not only its territory from others, but also its dishes.

This accusation is not entirely unfair, since falafel is of course much older than the Jewish state. The consensus among culinary historians is that the deep-fried balls originated in Egypt at least a thousand years ago. Yet still there are Israeli patriots who argue wide-eyed that falafel is a Jewish invention. According to them, it was Jewish slaves in biblical times who invented the dish. This seems fairly unlikely to me. According to the Bible, matzo was the main slave food in Egypt. When the Jewish people, in exile in the desert, lamented that everything was better in Egypt, they spoke of the meat stews and the bread – but not a word about the falafel.

On the other hand, falafel has always been a traditional part of the daily diet of the Sephardic Jews who emigrated to Israel from Islamic countries. They introduced falafel as street food and were the first to serve the balls in pittas. Unlike in Egypt and most Arab countries, they made their falafel from chickpeas instead of broad (fava) beans. Helped by the food shortages of the 1940s, their falafel became an immensely popular snack: it was cheap, nutritious and *parve* (both meat and dairy free), meaning that it could be eaten without any restrictions according to Jewish dietary laws (see page 313).

Although the modern state of Israel is a republic, many Israelis jokingly call their country a monarchy with reference to their beloved falafel stands. They typically have names like The Falafel King, The Real Falafel King, The New Falafel King, The King of Kings. Or The Falafel Queen, The Real Falafel Queen, The New... etc. The extent of Israeli devotion to falafel was demonstrated in 1959 by the band Ayalon. Their Shir Ha'Falafel ('The Falafel Song') has been covered many times:

No matter where in the world you go
you're sure to find dishes that you know
Even the youngest of kids are aware
that eating schnitzel is a Austrian affair
The French love to eat frogs
The Koreans grill their own dogs
Italians crave pasta by their grandmother
And cannibals? Well, they eat each other.

And we have falafel
Falafel, falafel
Our father's favourite bite
For mother a true delight
We'll have half a serving for grandma today
Even for mother-in-law we'll gladly pay
Falafel, falafel
with lots of chilli

Once, when a Jew arrived in Palestine
he'd kiss the ground and bless the Divine
When he gets off the plane today
he rushes out for falafel right away
We only have presidents, we have no monarchy
But the falafel stands are our own beloved royalty
Every day a new king is born
one 'happy', the other 'torn' *

'Cos we have falafel
Falafel, falafel
It's everyone's favourite treat
They sell it on every street
You can smell fried chickpeas everywhere
Its pungent aroma thickens the air
They all suffer from heartburn in Israel
From falafel, falafel
with lots and lots of chilli

Preparing falafel is not a piece of cake
It's something only true artists know to make
Every Yemenite Jew in the land of Israel
can judge its quality purely by smell
Even when hungry he will certainly refuse
falafel that was made by Ashkenazi Jews
Best to steer clear of such an ill-fated dish
as your falafel will taste of gefilte fish!

'Cos we have falafel
Falafel, falafel
Our father's favourite bite
For mother a true delight
And thus we must conclude
That this is our national food
Falafel, falafel
with lots and lots and lots of chilli

* In the 1950s a popular falafel stand in Tel Aviv was called
  Falafel Hameyu'ash, which translates as 'The Desperate Falafel'.
  Subsequently a competitor decided to name his stand Falafel
  Hame'ushar ('The Happy Falafel').

FALAFEL

Serves 10

2 × quantities tahini (page 282)
2 × quantities quick Israeli salad (page 291)
1 tablespoon TLV spice mix (page 288)
    or ras el hanout/baharat

500 g (1 lb 2 oz/2¼ cups) dried chickpeas
1 onion, chopped
4 garlic cloves
1 x large bunch flat-leaf (Italian) parsley
1 x large bunch coriander (cilantro)
1 jalapeño
2 tablespoons ground cumin
1 tablespoon ground coriander
1 teaspoon baking powder
2–3 teaspoons salt (to taste)
juice of 1 lemon
sunflower or peanut oil
10 pittas

The only tricky thing about falafel is that you have to soak the chickpeas well in advance. Most recipes suggest that you soak them overnight, but in my experience daylight works just as well – what's important is that you give them time. Never use tinned chickpeas to save time, because your falafel will fall apart as you fry them. A deep-fryer is handy here, but an ordinary heavy-based saucepan or frying pan also works well enough, especially in combination with a cooking thermometer. If possible, buy special falafel tongs – a kind of miniature ice-cream scoop. They will save you a lot of time and frustration, because good falafel batter is just too moist to easily roll into balls. If you don't have falafel tongs, then make quenelles of the batter using two dessert spoons.

Soak the chickpeas in plenty of cold water for 12 hours. Drain and blend to a fine – but not completely smooth – purée in a food processor. Transfer to a large bowl and set aside.

Purée the remaining ingredients (except the oil and pittas) and add the mixture to the chickpeas. Gradually pour in about 100 ml (3½ fl oz) of cold water and knead the mixture until smooth.

Preheat the oven to 100°C (210°F). Heat the oil to 180°C (350°F) in a deep-fryer or large, heavy-based saucepan or frying pan. Fry first a test falafel. Fill the falafel tongs with batter, smooth the top with a kitchen knife and lower it into the hot oil (or, make a quenelle of batter using two dessert spoons and lower it into the oil). Fry for 4–5 minutes, until lightly browned all over. Remove from the oil and, when cool enough to handle, taste. Add more salt or water to the remaining batter as necessary.

Fry the falafel balls in batches until golden brown. Remove from the oil and set aside to drain on a plate lined with paper towel. Keep warm in the oven while you make the rest.

Toast the pittas until hot but still soft. Cut each open and spread the inside with tahini. Fill each with some falafel balls and Israeli salad. If desired, serve with zhug (page 306), amba (page 307), chips (fries), and slices of red cabbage or gherkin.

200 g (7 oz/1¼ cups) blanched almonds
200 g (7 oz) caster (superfine) sugar
1 tablespoon orange-blossom water
pinch of salt
2 eggs
125 g (4½ oz/1 cup) raspberries
10 × frozen all-butter puff-pastry sheets
   (about 12 cm/5 in square)

RASPBERRY PUFF-PASTRY TARTS

Of course, nothing says 'special occasion' like a majestic, colourful, multi-layered cake. But if I've already committed myself to cooking a big meal, I prefer to keep things simple for dessert. In any case, if the main meal has gone to plan, by the time dessert arrives my guests will usually be happy with something modest. I often make these puff-pastry tarts. They can be prepared in five minutes flat and then you just pop them into the oven after you've cleared the starters. Minimum effort, maximum effect – guaranteed.

As a rule of thumb, assume half a tart per guest (allow a whole tart for gluttons). Make the tarts to order, as they taste best straight from the oven. Leftovers will keep in the fridge for up to two days.

Roughly chop the almonds in a food processor, then add the sugar, orange-blossom water, salt and 1 of the eggs and blend again until the mixture comes together as a sticky ball. Use your hands to work the raspberries roughly into the filling mixture (it should not be completely smooth). Cover and chill in the refrigerator until needed.

Preheat the oven to 200°C (400°F). Transfer the puff-pastry sheets from the freezer to the fridge so that they thaw a little, but not completely.

Remove only 1 puff-pastry sheet from the fridge at a time. Cut a 1 cm (½ in) strip from all four edges of the pastry. Stick the pastry strips on top of the puff-pastry sheet to make a raised border at the edge, pressing down to seal and cutting off any excess pastry at the corners. Brush the edge of this tart case with the beaten remaining egg. Fill the tart case with a little of the filling mixture. Repeat with the remaining puff-pastry sheets and filling mixture (or as needed).

Bake the puff-pastry tarts in the oven for 20–30 minutes, until the pastry is crisp and golden brown and the filling is springy to the touch. Cut in half diagonally and serve immediately, with the last drink of the evening.

ALL-CONCEALING BUREKAS

If you're a bit dyslexic, then perhaps you would think for a fraction of a second that this page is about burkas. Bu-re-kas (*burekasim* plural) is a hearty filled pastry related to the Turkish *börek*, the Bosnian *burek* and the Tunisian *brik*. However, for me it's not that strange to consider burkas and burekas on the same page.

For some time in the Netherlands it has been forbidden by law to wear face-covering clothing in public areas. This is a pure case of politicians playing to the gallery, because the number of women here who actually live their lives behind a veil is negligible. Things are very different in Israel – but even there, few Muslim women wear the burka. In Jaffa, the southern district of Tel Aviv, where more than one-third of the inhabitants are Arabs, I have never seen one. By contrast, the burkini is very popular. In Jaffa, to see a Muslim woman on the beach covered from head to toe is the most normal thing in the world. They share the sea with fellow citizens in skimpy, overtly sexy swimsuits and nobody raises an eyebrow.

In fact you're most likely to find women clad in full-body burkas – I kid you not – in the ultra-orthodox Jewish neighbourhoods of Jerusalem and the nearby Beit Shemesh. In this part of town, the robes are called 'frumkas', a contraction of 'frum' (Yiddish for 'pious') and 'burka'. I don't know the exact number of women who wear a frumka on a daily basis.
Let's just say there are far more Israeli frumkas than Dutch burkas – the former just don't get as much media attention as the latter.

As far as I've been able to verify, the words 'burekas' and 'burkas' are linguistically unrelated. Yet there is an essential similarity: the pastries popular in Israel hide their main ingredient from view. In order for customers to be able to recognise different burekas, each has a certain shape: the filling in a rectangular burekas is traditionally potato; a triangular burekas is usually filled with cheese; the half-moon-shaped pastries conceal a mushroom filling.

This useful system of categorisation has come under pressure in recent years. A growing number of creative bakers are turning their noses up at the traditional, somewhat boring fillings and cheerfully experimenting with more original flavour combinations. Now that the number of fillings exceeds the available number of geometric shapes, shape no longer provides any indication as to the filling inside. It's a development that could have caused tumult in only one country in the world.

This is how it works: Orthodox Jews aren't allowed to combine meat and dairy products – a supposedly biblical prohibition that is taken very seriously and interpreted rather rigidly. In order to be absolutely certain that a slow-moving beef croquette is not overtaken halfway along the digestive tract by a particularly agile cheese straw, the most devout consume no dairy products for six hours after eating meat. That's why the norm in Israel is for puff pastry to be made with (vegetable-based) margarine instead of butter: it allows both pious and non-observant citizens carefree enjoyment of a burekas at any time of the day. The exception, of course, is the cheese burekas – just as well it usually comes in the shape of a warning triangle ...

As more and more pastry chefs began to ignore the unwritten pastry laws, the chief rabbinate intervened. Nowadays, kosher businesses that sell a burekas in the 'wrong' shape instantly lose their accreditation. The same policy of zero tolerance has been applied to incorrectly designed croissants: those made with butter have to be shaped into the classic crescent shape; those made with margarine must be straight. Supervisors are employed to monitor compliance with this rabbinical decree.

Only in Israel.

30 g (1 oz) salted butter
1 teaspoon olive oil
1 large onion, chopped
1 garlic clove, grated or crushed
175 g (6 oz/3½ cups) English spinach
40 g (1½ oz/⅓ cup) grated parmesan
1 egg, separated
12 × frozen all-butter puff-pastry sheets
    (about 12 cm/5 in square)
1 tablespoon sesame seeds
1 tablespoon nigella seeds

SPINACH BUREKAS

Burekasim are everywhere in Israel, and are a fixture at weddings and bar- and bat-mitzvahs – a caterer without a burekas in his repertoire will not last long. If you're going to a friend's house to watch the football, you'll always bring beer and a takeaway bag of burekasim. These are usually of questionable quality. The puff pastry will be made with margarine to accommodate orthodox Jews (see page 75), while the overly salty fillings will contain plasticky cheese, potato powder or tinned mushrooms. If you're ever offered one, just for fun you should taste the filling on its own – it's a mystery how, when wrapped in pastry, they actually taste quite good.

Making your own burekasim is a piece of cake – and, of course, they taste much better. I make mine with all-butter puff pastry. You can make the puff pastry yourself, but it's a time-consuming task – and a thankless one, since the homemade pastry often doesn't taste any better than the factory-produced stuff.

Melt half of the butter and all of the oil in a large saucepan over low heat. Fry the onion and garlic for 5 minutes, or until softened. Add the spinach, increase the heat and continue to cook until wilted, stirring occasionally. Turn off the heat to medium and transfer the cooked spinach to a fine-mesh sieve suspended over another saucepan. Press the moisture from the spinach using the back of a wooden spoon, collecting the liquid in the second pan. Bring the liquid to the boil and reduce for 2–3 minutes, until nearly all the water has evaporated, then stir in the drained spinach, parmesan and the remaining butter. Set aside to cool for 1 minute, then beat in the egg yolk. When fully cooled, chill the filling mixure in the refrigerator.

Preheat the oven to 220°C (430°F). Remove the puff pastry from the freezer and place in the refrigerator so that it thaws slightly but not completely. Remove one sheet of puff pastry from the refrigerator at a time.

Whisk the egg white until frothy. Cut the first puff-pastry sheet in half and spoon a little of the filling mixture into the centre of each piece. Fold closed with your hands to form two parcels and crimp the edges with a fork. Brush each burekas with a little egg white and sprinkle with a few generous pinches of the sesame and nigella seeds. Repeat the process with the remaining puff-pastry sheets and filling mixture.

Bake the burekasim in the oven for 15–20 minutes, until crisp and golden brown. Cool for 10–15 minutes before serving.

Makes 24

50 g (1¾ oz/½ cup) grated parmesan
50 g (1¾ oz/⅓ cup) feta, crumbled
100 g (3½ oz) ricotta
1 teaspoon cornflour (cornstarch)
2 teaspoons za'atar
1 egg, separated
12 × frozen all-butter puff-pastry sheets
    (about 12 cm/5 in square)
2 tablespoons sunflower seeds

In a bowl, mix the parmesan, feta, ricotta and cornflour with 1 teaspoon of the za'atar and the egg yolk.

Preheat the oven to 220°C (430°F). Remove the puff pastry from the freezer and place in the refrigerator so that it thaws slightly but not completely. Remove one sheet of puff pastry from the refrigerator at a time.

Whisk the egg white until frothy. Cut the first puff-pastry sheet in half and spoon a little of the filling mixture into the centre of each piece. Fold closed with your hands to form two parcels and crimp the edges with a fork. Brush each burekas with a little egg white and sprinkle with a few generous pinches of the za'atar and sunflower seeds. Repeat the process with the remaining puff-pastry sheets and filling mixture.

Bake in the oven for 15–20 minutes, until crisp and golden brown. Cool for 10–15 minutes before serving.

THREE-CHEESE AND ZA'ATAR BUREKAS

After graduating from high school, I, like many of my classmates, left the Netherlands for a year out in Israel. At that time I was still in my pious period, so unlike most of my peers, who worked in kibbutzes, I chose to study in a yeshiva, a theological institute. There, my days were filled with the study of ancient religious texts. I turned out to have no natural affinity for this and was bored to death. My yeshiva was in Efrat, a remote hamlet south of Jerusalem. The nightlife in Efrat consisted of one mediocre pizzeria. I lived for Fridays, my only day of freedom: I would hitchhike to Jerusalem early in the morning to meet friends or just wander aimlessly around the shopping streets.

The last bus to Efrat left from the bus station an hour and a half before Shabbat. The first part of the journey was along Jaffa Road, at the time a ridiculously narrow street that was one of the busiest roads in the city – every bus heading south had to squeeze along it. My bus usually made such painfully slow progress that I could safely get off and grab a snack from Mahane Yehuda market.

On Friday afternoons it was a busy place, with swarms of people hurrying along, carrying their Shabbat groceries in thin plastic bags. At the crowded stops the buses took it in turns to pick up passengers, holding up all the traffic. Next to the bus stop was a stall selling burekasim. I can still remember the bittersweet smell of warm puff pastry mingled with the exhaust fumes of idling buses.

I never had to wait in line because the market vendor was my willing accomplice in this weekly ritual. He would slip me a paper bag so that I could fill it with cheese burekasim. Dark-brown grease stains would immediately appear on the outside of the bag, and I would pay him with the shekels that I had counted out in advance on the bus.

Every so often I would find the bus where I had left it and be able to get right back on. More often than not, I would have to run along the road to board at the next stop. Standing in the aisle of the overcrowded bus, I would eat the whole bag of burekasim in one go. The nausea usually lasted until Saturday afternoon.

BUREKAS WITH EXTRA-SMOKY EGGPLANT

Makes 24

2 eggplants (aubergines)
1½ teaspoons lapsang souchoung leaves
100 g (3½ oz/⅔ cup) feta, crumbled
1 egg, separated
pinch of salt
12 × frozen all-butter puff-pastry sheets
    (about 12 cm/5 in square), slightly thawed
1 tablespoon pepitas (pumpkin seeds)
1 teaspoon sumac

For a long time I've been searching for ways to get my *chatzilim al ha'eesj* – blackened eggplants (aubergines) – as smoky-tasting as those of even a third-rate Israeli home cook. Obviously, at first I tried copying whatever my friends and acquaintances did, but even then I couldn't work out their secret. There is no secret, they assured me time after time. I had to agree – they weren't doing anything that I hadn't tried before. The aubergines were flame-roasted on the gas stove until completely blackened, exactly as I cooked them at home. So why couldn't I get the flesh of my eggplants to taste like theirs?

I'm still not completely sure, but I suspect it has something to do with quality. In Israel, almost all available vegetables and fruit are locally grown. The sun is always shining and the harvest only takes place when the produce is ripe. If, like me, you've grown up with hot-housed fruit and vegetables, then when you first sink your teeth into an Israeli-grown grapefruit, avocado, tomato, strawberry or melon, it's a revelation. The locals aren't fussy about ugly-looking or misshapen produce, so perhaps what's on sale doesn't look as good as our produce, but it tastes far, far better. Man, I'm jealous of Israeli cooks, because having good ingredients is half the work.

This difference in quality is more difficult to discern with eggplants than with, say, tomatoes. After all, you never eat eggplants raw. Moreover, in the case of *chatzilim*, what you're looking for is not the eggplant with the tastiest flesh, but the eggplant that will best absorb the smoky flavour of the cooking process. Since Israeli crops are blessed not only with an abundance of sunlight, but also with just enough (rain) water to survive, their produce is less watery than ours. I suspect that this is why Israeli eggplants absorb smoky flavours so much better.

The good news is that I've come up with a trick to imbue second-rate eggplants with an intense smoky flavour. The magic ingredient is lapsang souchong, a Chinese tea whose leaves are dried over the embers of cypress wood. This process gives the tea its characteristic smoky taste, akin to that of peaty single-malt whisky. Mix the contents of a lapsang souchong teabag through the flesh of your blackened eggplants and yours will surpass even those of an Israeli cook.

Blacken the skin of the eggplants over the gas flame of your hob. If you don't have a gas stove, set your grill (broiler) to its highest setting and grill the eggplants until black on all sides (see page 299 for detailed instructions). Allow the eggplants to cool slightly, then scrape off the blackened skin. Cut the eggplants in half lengthways and scoop out the flesh. Drain the flesh in a fine-mesh sieve, squeezing out as much moisture as possible. Transfer the drained eggplant to a bowl and add the tea leaves, feta, egg yolk and a good pinch of salt. Mash until smooth.

Preheat the oven to 220°C (430°F). Whisk the egg white until frothy. Cut the first puff-pastry sheet in half and spoon a little of the filling mixture into the centre of each piece. Fold closed with your hands to form two parcels and crimp the edges with a fork. Brush each burekas with a little egg white and sprinkle with pepitas and a good pinch of sumac. Repeat the process with the remaining puff-pastry sheets and filling mixture.

Bake for 15–20 minutes, until crisp and golden brown. Cool for 10–15 minutes before serving.

THE MIGHTY, MEATY EGGPLANT

When it comes to eggplants (aubergines), an old Arabic adage is often wheeled out: 'Never marry a woman who doesn't have a hundred different recipes for eggplant.' Now, sharp Israeli tongues claim that Jews always exaggerate and Arabs always lie. However, for my money, that is itself a lie while the Arabic saying about eggplant is none other than a gross exaggeration. Doing a quick tally, I can only think of 25 eggplant recipes in my own repertoire. Granted, I'm neither an Arab nor a woman – but I'm definitely an eggplant fanatic.

In any case, everyone can agree that eggplants can be prepared in any number of ways. But to get the best out of them you must always heat them – preferably with a generous portion of fat. Raw eggplant is a punishment – and, apparently, unhealthy. By contrast, each cooking technique – frying, baking, roasting in the oven and grilling over an open fire – reveals a different, equally charming, side to the eggplant.

In fact, eggplants taste of very little. It's not their taste, but their tender, almost fleshy texture that makes them so popular. In the first years after the foundation of the state of Israel in 1948, when meat and poultry were scarce, the pioneers learned how to recreate the dishes they loved using eggplants as a substitute for meat. Every Israeli baby boomer grew up eating vegetarian chopped liver (see page 277), a pâté that replaced chicken livers with eggplants.

As prosperity increased, eggplants lost their function as a meat substitute. Government subsidies made chicken meat affordable to everyone and as a result, eggplant dishes fell out of favour – they reminded people too much of the lean years of yore. However, as with many childhood memories, in time the negativity associated with eggplants was replaced by nostalgia. In the nineties, vegetarian chopped liver experienced a revival thanks to an ageing generation of chefs wearing rose-tinted glasses.

The similarity between eggplant flesh and meat is particularly evident in sabich (page 40). This is one of those rare vegetarian dishes that can satisfy even the most committed carnivore. That's the magic quality of the mighty, meaty eggplant.

EGGPLANT SCHNITZELS

2 tablespoons plain (all-purpose) flour
2 eggs
35 g (1¼ oz/⅓ cup) dry breadcrumbs
    or 20 g (¾ oz/⅓ cup) Japanese
    breadcrumbs (panko)
2 tablespoons za'atar
1 tablespoon TLV spice mix (page 288)
    or ras el hanout/baharat
1 tablespoon sesame seeds
1 tablespoon nigella seeds
1 long, thin eggplant (aubergine)
coarse sea salt
sunflower or peanut oil for frying
3 tablespoons plain yoghurt
3 tablespoons raw tahini
2 mint sprigs, chopped
1 teaspoon lemon juice

The simplest way to prepare eggplant slices as if they were meat is to bread them and pan-fry them. According to Claudia Roden, the unsurpassed chronicler of Jewish cuisine, eggplant schnitzels have long been an important part of the Shabbat lunch in many Jewish communities. My mother serves them as a side dish on Friday evenings, before they've completely lost their crispness (after all, cooking is prohibited on Shabbat). They're at their best eaten lukewarm, just a few minutes after cooking.

Sprinkle the flour onto a large plate. Beat the eggs in a bowl. Mix the breadcrumbs, za'atar, spice mix, sesame seeds and nigella seeds and sprinkle onto a separate plate.

Slice the eggplant into thick rounds and season with salt. Dredge each eggplant slice first in the flour, then dip it in the beaten egg, then coat in the breadcrumb mixture.

Heat the oil in a large, heavy-based frying pan over medium–high heat – use enough oil to reach halfway up the eggplant slices. Fry the breaded eggplant slices for 3–4 minutes on each side, until the coating is golden brown and the eggplants are tender. Remove from the oil and drain on a plate lined with paper towel.

Just before serving, mix the yoghurt, tahini, mint and lemon juice, loosening it with a little water or milk if necessary. Serve the sauce alongside the eggplant schnitzels.

LIMONANA

Makes 4

150 g (5½ oz) granulated sugar
200 ml (7 fl oz) lemon juice (from
    about 3–4 lemons)
6 mint sprigs
400 g (14 oz/3 cups) ice cubes
450 ml (15 fl oz) sparkling mineral water

Tel Avivians are, by necessity, experts in heat control: summers are long and clammy and life is too short for slowing down. The importance of staying hydrated goes without saying, but the people you see roaming around in the sweltering heat carrying bottles of water are usually tourists; locals prefer to quench their thirst with freshly squeezed fruit juice. Small kiosks, their serving hatches bedecked with tropical fruit, meet this need – here you can order smoothies or juices made with whatever fruit you want and mixed with crushed ice.

The most popular thirst-quencher is without a doubt *limonana*. This is not Hebrew for 'lemonade', as I wrongly assumed for years, but a contraction of its two main ingredients: *limon* ('lemon') and *nana* ('mint'). Be aware that in certain places, such as beach shacks or restaurants, the limonana will probably be bought in rather than made to order. You'll be able to tell the soft drink from the real thing by its colour: freshly made limonana is green from the mint leaves – and, it goes without saying, much more delicious.

You can use this recipe to make ice lollies, too: add 50 g (1¾ oz) of extra sugar, replace the sparkling mineral water with regular water and leave out the ice cubes. Or give your limonana an alcoholic kick with a good dash of arak to turn it into ... *limonanarak!*

Pour 250 ml (8½ fl oz/1 cup) water into a heavy-based saucepan and stir in the sugar. Bring the mixture to the boil, stirring until the sugar has dissolved. Set aside to cool, then chill in the refrigerator for at least 1 hour, until cold.

Blend the chilled sugar water, lemon juice, mint leaves and ice cubes until the ice is crushed. Divide the mixture equally among four tall glasses and top up with the mineral water.

VEGAN CAULIFLOWER SHAWARMA

In Israel, shawarma is often eaten in a wrap instead of a pitta; the meat and salads are wrapped in laffa. TV chef Barak Yehezkeli, the main man at restaurant Burek, invented a vegan version of this dish by swapping the laffa for iceberg lettuce and the meat for chargrilled cauliflower. It's a typical Tel Avivian invention: simple, original, and testament to all the good stuff the country has to offer.

Roll the chilli back and forth between your palms to release the seeds. Slice the chilli into thin rings, shaking out the seeds. Mix the chilli with the rocket, herbs, onions and almonds, then stir in the lemon juice and extra virgin olive oil and season with a generous pinch of sea salt.

Cut the cauliflower into thick slices, and cut the slices into 2 cm (¾ in) wide strips. Add enough oil to a large, heavy-based frying pan to reach halfway up the cauliflower pieces. Fry the cauliflower pieces, in batches if necessary, over medium–high heat until golden brown on both sides. Remove from the hot oil and drain on paper towel. Season with salt.

Divide the fried cauliflower and salad among the 4 lettuce leaves. Drizzle with tahini, then eat (in spite of the photo) without cutlery.

Serves 4

1 red chilli
6 rocket (arugula) leaves, roughly chopped
6 coriander (cilantro) sprigs, leaves roughly chopped
6 mint sprigs, roughly chopped
6 oregano sprigs, roughly chopped
3 spring onions (scallions), green parts thickly sliced
1 small red onion, chopped
50 g (1¾ oz/⅓ cup) unsalted roasted almonds, roughly chopped
juice of 1 small lemon
dash of extra virgin olive oil
coarse sea salt
1 cauliflower, leaves removed
olive oil for frying
4 iceberg lettuce leaves (not the outermost ones)
4 tablespoons raw tahini

4 eggs
1 tablespoon mayonnaise
1 tablespoon crème fraîche
1 tablespoon harissa
1 teaspoon za'atar
½ teaspoon paprika
1 teaspoon lemon juice
pinch of salt
1 tablespoon sesame seeds
1 tablespoon nigella seeds

DEVILLED EGGS

In English, stuffed eggs are called 'devilled eggs'. I've always found this a bit over the top for what is perhaps the most petit-bourgeois of all snacks. My stuffed eggs, however, deserve to be called devils. They look innocent enough, but they contain an infernally hot twist in the form of za'atar and spicy harissa.

Boil the eggs for 10 minutes, then drain and run under cold water until cool enough to handle. Peel the eggs and cut each in half lengthways. Pop out the yolks using your thumb and mash them in a bowl with a fork until smooth (reserve the whites). Stir in the mayonnaise, crème fraîche, harissa, za'atar, paprika and lemon juice. Season with a pinch of salt.

Sprinkle the sesame seeds and nigella seeds onto a plate. Press the cut sides of each egg into the seed mixture, then fill with the spiced egg mayonnaise. If you don't want to fiddle about with teaspoons of filling here, invest in a piping bag with a fluted nozzle – it gives the eggs an old-school look that's so wrong it's right.

CHEESE STRAWS WITH ZA'ATAR, PINE NUTS, SESAME AND NIGELLA SEEDS

Makes 14

60 g (2 oz) pine nuts
25 g (1 oz) sesame seeds
25 g (1 oz) nigella seeds
6 × frozen all-butter puff-pastry
    sheets (about 12 cm/5 in square)
plain (all-purpose) flour for
    dusting
1 egg, beaten
2 tablespoons za'atar
80 g (2¾ oz) unaged gouda, finely
    grated

My father is crazy about the cheese straws from Tel Aviv's Lehamim bakery. During the parts of the year that he and my mother spend in their apartment in Tel Aviv, the city's best bakery cranks up its cheese-straw production a couple of notches to cater to Mr Krant's addiction. Now, although the cheese straws at Lehamim are, like everything it produces, indescribably delicious, there's nothing Israeli about them. In fact, in *Breaking Breads*, the bakery's beautiful cookbook, owner Uri Scheft reveals the secret of his cheese straws to be none other than unaged Dutch gouda. According to Scheft, Dutch cheese has the optimal balance between spicy and sweet and melts better than aged cheeses such as parmesan and pecorino. That's probably the reason my father is so fond of them: they remind him of home. Because I'm always trying to cure my homesickness for Tel Aviv with food, I devised these cheese straws made with za'atar, pine nuts, sesame seeds, nigella seeds and... yes, unaged gouda.

Preheat the oven to 220°C (430°F). Dry-fry the pine nuts until lightly golden brown (keep your eye on them as they toast in the pan as they will burn easily). Using a mortar and pestle pound the pine nuts to a sticky paste. Mix the sesame seeds and nigella seeds in a bowl.

Just before you need them, remove 3 sheets of puff pastry from the freezer to defrost a little (if you leave them out too long they will be too sticky to work with). Dust your work surface with flour and roll out each puff-pastry sheet until it has doubled in length.

Cover one of the rolled-out puff-pastry sheets with half of the crushed pine nuts. Top with a second rolled-out puff-pastry sheet and press down. Brush the top of that sheet with beaten egg and sprinkle all over with 1 tablespoon of the za'atar.

Brush both sides of the third rolled-out puff-pastry sheet with more beaten egg and press it down on top of the other two. Sprinkle all over with half of the sesame/nigella-seed mixture.

Turn the puff-pastry stack over then brush the top with more beaten egg. Top with half of the grated cheese and press down well.

Trim the edges of the puff-pastry stack with a sharp knife or pizza roller. Transfer to a baking tray and chill in the freezer for 3–5 minutes.

Meanwhile, repeat the process with the remaining puff-pastry sheets and filling ingredients.

Cut each puff-pastry stack lengthways into 7 thin strips, then twist each strip into a spiral. Arrange the cheese-straw spirals onto a baking tray lined with baking paper, pressing the ends of each onto the baking paper to prevent them untwisting.

Bake the cheese straws in the oven for 10–12 minutes, until lightly golden brown (too dark and they will taste bitter). Serve lukewarm or wait until they have completely cooled.

PITTA BRUSCHETTA

Serves 6

3 pittas
extra virgin olive oil
1 garlic clove, cut in half

Serving your guests an unfinished sandwich – it's something the Italians have been getting away with since time immemorial by calling it *bruschetta*. Now the rest of the world has got in on the act. After all, sandwiches are easy to make, and *bruschetta* has the added advantage of reminding everyone who has ever spent an unforgettable week in Tuscany of their holidays.

Traditionally, *bruschetta* was a tasty way of using up odds and ends from the bread bin. Obviously, it's not quite the same when you're running a restaurant or preparing for a houseful of guests. Nor is it the same when the bread we lesser mortals usually have left over is from a processed, sliced loaf. We're more likely to buy a rustic artisan loaf four times the price of our usual bread specifically to make *bruschetta* – we'll use what we need and let the rest go stale in the bread bin. In other words: the exact opposite.

I make my *bruschetta* out of pitta halves. There are many up sides to doing it this way: unlike ciabatta, pittas have no holes, so you don't have to worry about gravity dispensing with your topping. Another advantage is that pittas remain crisp even with the moistest of toppings. Pittas are also thinner, and therefore less filling, than a slice of normal bread, so they won't spoil your guests' appetites before the main course. Moreover, I for one always have pittas to hand. Even if I think I've run out, I'll inevitably find some forgotten stock hidden in the freezer behind some lamb shoulder or other slab of meat.

Preheat your oven to its hottest setting and switch on the grill (broiler). Toast the pittas in a toaster until they curl slightly. Using a sharp knife, cut each pitta in half around the edge to make two thin discs (take care as hot steam will escape from inside the pittas). Brush the rough side of each pitta half with a little of the oil, then place them oil-side up directly under the grill. Grill for 1–2 minutes, until crisp and lightly golden brown. Don't take your eyes off them, because the difference between a perfectly toasted pitta and a miserably cremated one is a matter of seconds.

Rub the cut edge of each pitta with the cut half of the garlic clove. Drizzle the pittas with a little more oil. Add your toppings and serve immediately.

For toppings, see pages 98–103.

350 g (12½ oz/1¾ cups)
    deseeded and finely diced
    vine tomatoes
1 small red chilli, deseeded
    and finely chopped
3 garlic cloves, crushed
    or finely chopped
8 fresh za'atar sprigs
    (or oregano), chopped
extra virgin olive oil
salt and freshly ground
    black pepper
3 pittas

PITTA BRUSCHETTA WITH TOMATO AND ZA'ATAR (OR OREGANO)

I love all fresh herbs, but if I could only grow one, I'd definitely choose za'atar. The intense, peppery aroma is slightly acidic and the flavour is delightfully musty. With za'atar, it's not usually a case of love at first bite. However, as often happens with more challenging flavours, you'll eventually fall madly in love with it. Unfortunately, fresh za'atar is extremely scarce, even in Israel. Wild za'atar is threatened with extinction and by law can no longer be picked; cultivated za'atar almost always ends up in a dried-herb mix.

Fresh oregano is an excellent alternative to fresh za'atar. Strangely enough, depending on where you live in the world, that too is often hard to come by. Where I live, many supermarkets do not sell oregano. I usually go to the greengrocer, but the quality of oregano that I find there can vary considerably. Good-quality oregano has small leaves with a velvety texture. While no one's looking, take a leaf of your greengrocer's oregano and bite into it: if its flavour is sharp enough to make the tip of your tongue tingle, then it's the real deal.

Mix the tomatoes, chilli, garlic and za'atar with a generous splash of the oil and season to taste with salt and freshly ground black pepper. Cover and set aside for at least 30 minutes at room temperature so that the flavours can develop.

Cut the pittas in half around the edges to create two flat discs from each. Toast under the grill (broiler) until golden brown (see page 97). Top the pitta bruschetta with the tomato salsa and serve immediately.

Above left: pita bruschetta with matboecha, goat cheese and leaves of oregano.

100 g (3½ oz/¾ cup) pepitas
    (pumpkin seeds)
15 g (½ oz) fresh mint
juice of ½ small lemon
extra virgin olive oil
salt and freshly ground black pepper
3 pittas
handful of rocket (arugula)
125 g (4½ oz) buffalo mozzarella, torn
2 tablespoons pomegranate seeds

PITTA BRUSCHETTA WITH MOZZARELLA, MINT PESTO AND POMEGRANATE SEEDS

The combination of pepitas and fresh mint with olive oil and a little lemon juice creates a deliciously fresh pesto that matches perfectly with mozzarella and pomegranate seeds. The result resembles a caprese salad – the classic combination of mozzarella, tomato and basil – but tastes completely different.

Dry-fry the pepitas over medium heat until they start to pop in the pan – but don't let them brown. Transfer the seeds to the bowl of a food processor and set aside to cool, then blitz them with the mint leaves. Gradually add the lemon juice and olive oil to the mixture until it forms a smooth pesto. Season to taste with salt and freshly ground black pepper.

Cut the pittas in half around the edges to create two flat discs from each. Toast under the grill (broiler) until golden brown (see page 97). Top the bruschetta with the rocket, mozzarella and pesto and sprinkle over the pomegranate seeds. Serve immediately.

Photo on previous page.

PITTA BRUSCHETTA WITH PLENTY OF 'MMM!'

Serves 6

6 roasted garlic bulbs (page 286)
120 g (4½ oz/⅓ cup) caramelised onions
   (page 287)

2 tablespoons garlic oil
500 g (1 lb 2 oz) white button mushrooms,
   cleaned with paper towel and quartered
4 anchovy fillets in olive oil, drained and
   finely chopped
dash of Campari
6 thyme sprigs
dash of extra virgin olive oil
salt and freshly ground white pepper
3 pittas

In addition to the four basic tastes – sweet, salt, sour and bitter – there is another, lesser known basic taste: umami. It was first discovered by a Japanese professor researching seaweed – that's why we ended up with a Japanese name for it. According to people who speak better Japanese than I do, *umami* can be roughly translated as 'mmm!'. The taste of umami is one of intense savouriness – it acts as a kind of culinary catalyst, giving extra oomph to the other basic tastes. The ingredient that causes this taste sensation is glutamate, an amino acid found in high concentration in ingredients including garlic, anchovies, mushrooms, caramelised onions, sun-dried tomatoes, soy sauce and parmesan.

What makes umami so fantastic is that you can literally never have too much of it. A dish can be deemed too salty, too sweet, too bitter or too acidic, but never 'too umami'. Don't believe me? This pitta bruschetta with plenty of 'mmm!' will convince you.

Heat the garlic oil in a frying pan over high heat. Add the mushrooms and a generous pinch of salt and fry for 8–10 minutes, stirring regularly. Add the anchovies and Campari and continue to cook until most of the moisture has evaporated.

Transfer the mushroom mixture to a plastic container with a lid. Stir in the thyme leaves and oil, and season to taste with salt and freshly ground white pepper. Close the lid and set aside for at least 1 hour to marinate.

Cut the pittas in half around the edges to create two flat discs from each. Toast under the grill (broiler) until golden brown (see page 97). Squeeze the roasted garlic from its skin and spread over the bruschetta, then spoon the caramelised onions on top. Top with the mushrooms. Serve immediately.

Photograph on page 99.

PITTA BRUSCHETTA WITH COTTAGE CHEESE AND ZA'ATAR

Serves 6

3 pittas
200 g (7 oz) cottage cheese
2 tablespoons za'atar
extra virgin olive oil

Cut the pittas in half around the edges to create two flat discs from each. Toast under the grill (broiler) until golden brown (see page 97). Spread each bruschetta with cottage cheese, then sprinkle generously with za'atar and drizzle with olive oil. Serve immediately.

Photograph on page 99.

Israelis cannot live without cottage cheese. This may sound strange, because the lumpy, Quark-like cheese is something most people associate with a continental breakfast in a Tyrolean ski chalet rather than with a sunny Israeli meal. Yet an Israeli breakfast without *hüttenkäse* is as weird as Passover without matzo. The extent of Israeli devotion to cottage cheese was (quite literally) demonstrated in 2011 when the cheese was at the centre of mass demonstrations that lasted for months.

While shopping for the Jewish holiday of Shavuot – a celebration that traditionally involves a lot of cheese – a young orthodox man discovered that the price of *hüttenkäse* had increased by 40 percent in a very short time. On Facebook he called for a boycott of all soft white cheeses (in Israel, most of these are produced by the same manufacturer). The response was huge: people's latent anger about the sky-high cost of living suddenly boiled over.

About a month before the Occupy protests broke out worldwide, hundreds of demonstrators had already pitched their tents along Tel Aviv's Rothschild Boulevard. Soon the 'tentifada' had spread to the rest of the country. Every weekend, hundreds of thousands of people took to the streets to demand affordable rent, free childcare and other social reforms. And that's how the *hüttenkäse* boycott caused the largest socio-economic uprising in Israeli history.

Eventually, the protests died a silent death – the media lost interest and the protesters decided that they wanted their relaxed weekends back. The government dismantled the protesters' camps and promised various socio-economic reforms, but ultimately little changed. Yet the protests were not a complete failure: Israeli dairy manufacturers duly and permanently reduced the price of their cottage cheese.

Makes 50

4 tablespoons salted peanuts
1 tablespoon silan or date syrup
200 g (7 oz) dark chocolate (maximum 50% cocoa)
175 g (6¼ oz/⅔ cup) raw tahini
icing (confectioners') sugar for dredging

TAHINI AND CHOCOLATE TRUFFLES

This is by far the simplest dessert in this book, but no one needs to know that. Serve these to your guests in a nonchalant way and I promise they'll think you are the winner of *The Great British Bake Off*. Don't use extra-dark chocolate for these – you'll get the best results with a bog-standard bar made with 50 percent cocoa. On the other hand, the tahini you use must be of the very best quality.

Preheat the oven to 180°C (350°F). Line a baking tray with baking paper. Scatter the peanuts over the tray and roast in the oven for 8–10 minutes, until golden brown (keep your eye on them to prevent them from burning). Remove from the oven and drizzle with the silan or date syrup. Set aside to cool.

Line a small square cake tin with plastic wrap. Melt the chocolate in a bain-marie or in the microwave. As soon as the chocolate has melted, stir in the tahini and peanuts, then pour the mixture into the prepared cake tin. Set aside to cool, then chill in the refrigerator for at least 3 hours.

Sprinkle icing sugar onto a plate. Using a sharp kitchen knife, cut the hardened *chocola-tini* into cubes, then dredge each cube in the icing sugar. Keep in the refrigerator until ready to serve (if left at room temperature for too long, they will become gooey).

ZA'ATAR OMELETTE
IN A PITTA

Serves 1

Pittas are the ideal bread in which to sandwich a hasty takeaway breakfast. However, you must still watch out for the sauce dripping from the pitta – make sure it ends up on the pavement and not your clothes …

1 tablespoon tahini (page 282)

2 eggs
3 tablespoons crème fraîche
2 teaspoons za'atar
2 pinches of salt
knob of butter
8 cherry tomatoes, halved
1 spring onion (scallion), roughly
   chopped
extra virgin olive oil
1 large pitta
1 coriander (cilantro) sprig, leaves
   coarsely chopped

Beat the eggs in a bowl with the crème fraîche and za'atar. The mixture doesn't need to be smooth. Season with a pinch of salt.

Heat the butter in a small frying pan, ideally one that has a lid and is no bigger than a pitta. Fry the omelette, covered, over low heat, until it has risen considerably and is almost cooked through (the top of the omelette will be opaque).

Meanwhile, fry the tomatoes and over high heat in a small dry frying pan. Shake the pan regularly and stir with a spatula to prevent the tomatoes from sticking to the bottom. Continue to cook the tomatoes until they are beginning to blacken, then add the spring onion and a pinch of salt. Fry for a further 30 seconds, then stir in a small splash of the olive oil.

Turn the omelette over and cook for a further 30 seconds over medium heat. Remove from the pan and set aside.

Toast the pitta for a few seconds until it is hot but not crisp. Cut the pitta open and smear the insides generously with tahini. Fill the pitta with the omelette, the tomato-and-onion mixture, and a sprinkling of coriander, then drizzle with the tahini.

55 g (2 oz/⅓ cup) poppy seeds
55 g (2 oz/⅓ cup) sesame seeds
55 g (2 oz/⅓ cup) roasted almonds
150 g (5½ oz/⅔ cup) caster (superfine)
   sugar
1 egg, plus 1 egg white
1 tablespoon rosewater
pinch of salt
14 filo pastry sheets (or spring-roll
   wrappers)
sunflower or peanut oil for deep-frying
1 tablespoon pistachios, finely chopped
2 tablespoons honey

SIGARIM SPICED WITH POPPY SEEDS, SESAME SEEDS AND ALMONDS

Sigarim – deep-fried cigars of filo pastry filled with spiced minced (ground) meat – was brought to the region by North African immigrants, and is as popular and indispensable here as *bitterballen* are in the Netherlands. I have sat through countless Israeli weddings (including my own) and I have yet to attend one that doesn't serve *sigarim*. *Sigarim* are more versatile than *bitterballen* because they can be filled with sweet ingredients as well as savoury fillings such as meat, cheese or vegetables.

To make the sweet filling of this recipe you'll need a special poppy-seed mill. Don't let that put you off, because they're easy to come by and look charmingly old-fashioned. Think of it as an investment – the mills are also suitable for grinding spices, meaning that you can start making your own spice blends (see page 288).

Use a poppy-seed mill to grind the poppy and sesame seeds. Transfer the ground seeds to the bowl of a food processor and add the almonds, sugar, whole egg, rosewater and salt. Blend until the mixture comes together as a sticky dough.

Work with one sheet of filo pastry (or spring-roll wrapper) at a time to prevent them from drying out. Cut the pastry into a 16 cm (6¼ in) square using a sharp knife or pizza roller. Take a tablespoon of the filling mixture, roll it into a sausage shape using your hands, and line it up with the bottom of the pastry square (the filling should be short enough to leave 2 cm/¾ in of pastry free at each side). Whisk the egg white in a bowl until frothy and brush the top of the square and the sides with a little of it. Working from the bottom edge of the square to the top, roll the pastry around the filling, then twist the ends closed like a boiled sweet.

Heat enough oil in a heavy-based saucepan to completely cover the sigarim. When the oil reaches 180°C (350°F), lower the sigarim into it in batches and fry until the pastry is crisp and pale golden brown. (Do not fry the sigarim for too long, because they can explode.) Using a sharp knife, trim the ends of the sigarim to reveal the filling.

Grind the pistachios in the poppy-seed mill. Arrange the sigarim on a platter and drizzle over the honey, then sprinkle with the ground pistachios. Serve the sigarim lukewarm or at room temperature.

PITTA WITH SEA BREAM AND SAMPHIRE

I couldn't seem to come up with a good recipe for a fish pitta. The pitta had to contain balls, of that I was certain. The balls had to be crisp on the outside and creamy on the inside – like falafel, but using fish instead of chickpeas. I tried countless variations; I experimented with fresh fish, frozen fish, tinned fish; I baked, grilled and deep-fried them. Whatever I tried, a eureka moment was not forthcoming. As soon as the fish balls were tucked into a warm pitta and topped with a dollop of tahini, they disintegrated to mush. It was always tasty, but never cookbook appropriate.

So I shelved the balls and carried on with my life, until one day I unthinkingly stuffed some of the kids' left-over fish fingers into a pitta for a quick snack. Suddenly: eureka! I realised that my obsession with fish balls had blinded me to the possibility of filling a pitta with crisp-skinned fried fish! It turned out to be a big hit.

Sea bream (also known as dorade) is one of the most popular fish in Tel Aviv's restaurants. On Israeli menus it's known as *denis* (and pronounced the same as in the Blondie song). If you can't find sea bream, you could also use sea bass for this recipe.

Serves 2

½ × quantity tahini (page 282)

2 × 125 g (4½ oz) sea bream fillets, skin on
extra virgin olive oil
sea salt flakes and freshly ground black pepper
4 flat-leaf (Italian) parsley sprigs, finely chopped with a sharp knife
25 g (1 oz) fresh samphire
1 spring onion (scallion), green part thinly sliced into rings
1 small green chilli, deseeded and thinly sliced into rings
2 large pittas

Rub the fish fillets all over with the oil and sprinkle a little salt over the skin of each. Spread the parsley leaves onto a chopping board and grind a generous amount of black pepper over them.

Blanch the samphire in a saucepan of boiling water for 2 minutes. Drain in a colander, then suspend the colander over the still-warm pan.

Meanwhile, heat a chargrill pan or heavy-based frying pan over high heat. When the pan is smoking hot, chargrill the sea bream fillets, skin-side down, for 3–4 minutes, until the edges of the fish fillets turn opaque and white. Turn the fillets over and cook for a further 1–2 minutes, until just cooked through. (If the skin sticks to the pan, gently pull it from the fish and set aside with the parsley on the chopping board.)

Lay the fish fillets on the chopping board, skin-side up. Cut into strips using a sharp knife. Scatter with the samphire, spring onion and chilli, and drizzle with more olive oil.

Toast the pittas until hot but still soft. Cut them open and spread the insides generously with tahini. Transfer everything on the chopping board to the pitta and serve immediately with a glass of minerally white wine.

RATATOUILLE PITTA

1 × quantity tahini (page 282)
1 × quantity zhug (page 306)

1 eggplant (aubergine), cut into large cubes
salt
2 red or yellow capsicums (bell peppers)
1 large onion, roughly chopped
3 garlic cloves, roughly chopped
olive oil for frying
1 zucchini (courgette), diced
400 g (14 oz) tin tomatoes
4 thyme sprigs
4 rosemary sprigs
salt and freshly ground black pepper
pinch sugar (optional)
2 eggs
4 pittas

The menu of Tel Aviv's pitta-based restaurant Miznon (a laminated affair written in felt-tip pen and covered with animal stickers) has two sections: on the left you'll find pittas with meaty fillings; on the right are vegetarian options. Unless you're a vegetarian, it's rather difficult to get beyond that first column, because everything in it will make your mouth water. Still, I recommend that, at least once, you skip the delicious minute steak, steak 'n' egg, lamb kebab, chicken livers and slow-stewed beef fillings in favour of the ratatouille pitta, whose combination of silky vegetables, creamy tahini and warm bread is a match made in heaven.

This dish takes a while to make, but it's ideal if you're catering for a large group, because it improves in flavour if left in the fridge overnight. Make it the day before your gathering and you'll be able to join your friends in an apéritif when they arrive rather than slaving in the kitchen. The only drawback is that the day before you'll need to dedicate at least an hour to frying all of the vegetables separately. Don't try to speed things up by randomly slicing vegetables into the same pan, because you'll end up with a soggy vegetable purée. If you don't have three pans, cook each vegetable one after another in the same pan – this requires more time but saves on washing up.

Sprinkle the eggplant cubes generously with salt and set aside for 20 minutes.

Meanwhile, blacken the capsicums over the open flame of your gas hob, or under a grill (broiler) set to its highest setting (see instructions on page 298). When the skin is completely blackened and beginning to flake, transfer the capsicums to zip-lock bags, seal and set aside to cool.

Fry the onion and garlic in a little olive oil over low heat. In a separate pan, fry the zucchini in a little olive oil over low heat. When the surface of the eggplant cubes is moist, brush away the excess salt and fry them in oil in a third frying pan. Stir the contents of each pan every now and again.

Scrape the blackened skin from the capsicums, then cut in half and remove the stalk and seeds. Chop the flesh and add it to the pan containing the onion.

When the onion mixture, zucchini and eggplant are soft and golden brown, combine them all in the largest pan, add the tomatoes and break the tomatoes up with a spatula. Tie the thyme and rosemary sprigs with cooking string and add to the pan. Bring the mixture to a gentle simmer and simmer for 40 minutes, stirring regularly. Remove the herbs and season to taste with salt and freshly ground black pepper – and possibly a pinch of sugar (or a squirt of tomato ketchup). Set aside in a cool place to let the flavours develop (or cool then chill in the refrigerator overnight). Taste and season again before serving.

Just before serving, boil the eggs for 10 minutes. Meanwhile, slowly warm the ratatouille over low heat, stirring regularly. Drain the eggs and run them under cold water until cool enough to handle, then peel and cut in half. Toast the pittas until hot but still soft. Slice the top off each pitta, spread the insides generously with tahini, then fill with ratatouille. Crumble half an egg into each pitta to garnish, plus a little more tahini and zhug if desired.

CHREMZELS

These sweet donuts made from crumbled matzo can be made in an instant and are very tasty, but I only ever make them once a year because they're so inextricably linked to Passover (see page 313) that it doesn't occur to me to put them on the table at any other time. For me, eating chremzels in December is like eating Easter eggs at Christmas. But you're free to make them any time you want to.

Some people shallow-fry their chremzels as flat biscuits. This method saves on oil (and probably quite a few calories). However, I prefer to fry them as dumplings, because I think they taste better and – the reason that trumps all others – because my mother and grandmother also cooked them this way.

100 g (3½ oz) raisins
350 g (12½ oz) matzo
100 ml (3½ fl oz) sweet red wine (about 15% abv)
5 large eggs
150 g (5½ oz) granulated sugar
1 teaspoon ground cinnamon
grated zest of 1 lemon
100 g (3½ oz/⅔ cup) roasted almonds, finely chopped
1 granny smith (or other tart green apple), peeled, cored and chopped into small pieces
2–3 tablespoons matzo meal (or dried breadcrumbs)
sunflower or peanut oil for deep-frying
icing (confectioners') sugar for dusting

Soak the raisins in a bowl of boiling water for 10 minutes, then drain and squeeze out the moisture.

Crumble the matzo into shards in a large bowl. Add the wine, raisins, eggs, granulated sugar, cinnamon, lemon zest, almonds, apple and matzo meal and beat to a sticky but firm batter using a wooden spoon (or your hands). Gradually add extra matzo meal if the batter is too sloppy. Using wet hands, roll ping-pong-sized balls from the batter.

Heat the oil in a deep, heavy-based saucepan to 180°C (350°F), or until a breadcrumb sizzles and turns golden brown when dropped into it. The oil should be deep enough to cover the donuts. Lower the donuts into the hot oil, in batches if necessary, and fry until golden brown. Remove from the pan using a slotted spoon and set aside to drain on paper towel.

Dust the donuts with icing sugar and serve lukewarm.

Serves 4–6

2 tablespoons TLV spice mix (page 288)
   or ras el hanout/baharat

40 g (1½ oz/¼ cup) pine nuts
1 kg (2 lb 3 oz) minced (ground) lamb
   or mutton
1 large onion, finely chopped
4 garlic cloves, crushed
1 tablespoon harissa
25 g (1 oz) flat-leaf (Italian) parsley, finely
   chopped
4–6 long cinnamon sticks

Prepare your barbecue well in advance.

Dry-fry the pine nuts until golden
brown, shaking the pan regularly and
keeping your eye on the nuts – they
burn quickly. Roughly chop.

In a large bowl, mix together the lamb,
pine nuts, onion, garlic, harissa, TLV
spice and parsley. If the fat content of
the meat is too low, add a tablespoon of
fat, such as schmaltz (page 308), to the
mix – after your hands have finished
mixing, they should feel as if you've
just smeared your whole family with
sunscreen.

Shape the meat mixture around the
cinnamon sticks to form shish kebabs.
Grill on the hot barbecue (or cook in a
chargrill pan) for 10 minutes, or until
the meat is completely cooked through.

The shish kebabs go well with hummus,
tahini (page 282), baba ghanoush or
quick Israeli salad (page 291).

SHISH KEBABS ON CINNAMON STICKS

One of the first things that *olim chadashim* (new immigrants) notice about Israelis is their deep-seated passion for their *mangal*, or barbecue. That love is shared by everyone in the country, regardless of race, class or religion; *al ha'esh* (literally, 'on the fire') is Israel's only national sport, and it brings everyone – Jew or Arab, Ashkenazi or Sephardic, young or old, carnivore or vegan – together. Astronauts looking down on the Levant from their spaceship on any Israeli national holiday would be forgiven for thinking that a volcano had erupted.

The smoke from all that collective barbecueing is thickest on Yom Ha'atzmaut, Israel's Independence Day (which takes place in late April or early May). That's when half the country heads to one of the national parks, the boot of their car stuffed with a portable mangal and cool boxes containing far too much food for just one day. Traditionally on this day, people would enjoy a long walk before unfolding the picnic blanket; nowadays, many people skip the hike and flop down in the first nice green field they find. In fact, some don't even make it out of the car park, and celebrate their independence on the tarmac right next to their car.

Obviously it's extremely difficult to persuade anyone from Tel Aviv to forsake their city to do battle with traffic jams in the provinces. Instead many set up their mangals in one of the city's parks or celebrate with a barbecue on the beach. You won't find steak or other fancy meat on the average Tel Avivian barbecue – for rib-eye you go to a restaurant. When it comes to mangals, cheap barbecue meat is the order of the day – a hangover from the first decades after the founding of the state, when meat was so scarce and expensive that Israelis used sauces and marinades to make minced meat, chicken thighs and sausages taste special.

I came up with the idea for this recipe on Alma Beach, in Jaffa. It was there that I saw an Arab family eating meat threaded not onto metal skewers but onto long cinnamon sticks. This technique gives the kebabs a delicious smoky cinnamon flavour that marries very well with lamb. If you can't find cinnamon sticks that are long enough, make drumstick-style mini-kebabs using regular cinnamon sticks.

AT THE TABLE

DOK'S ROASTED KOHLRABI

Serves 4

4 kohlrabi (about 180 g/6¼ oz each), leaves and stalks removed
best-quality mild extra virgin olive oil
coarse sea salt
1 green chilli, deseeded and finely diced
handful of fresh young thyme sprigs
100 g (3½ oz/⅔ cup) feta, crumbled
1 tablespoon sesame seeds or poppy seeds

There can't be more than eight bar stools and two bistro tables in Dok, undoubtedly Tel Aviv's most petite restaurant. There are also a few tables outside on the pavement, but the best spot is at the bar, where chef-patron Asaf Doktor watches over you. With minimal means – there's no space for decent kitchen equipment – the chef produces one bewitching dish after another (mostly prepped earlier that day in the kitchen of his flagship, Ha'achim, just down the street).

Asaf Doktor does everything just a little differently. He didn't seek to cash in on the success of Ha'achim by turning it into a chain. Instead, he opened a new postage stamp–sized restaurant with a mission: to work only with locally sourced ingredients. Not in a half-hearted way, like so many restaurants that make a big fuss every time they have a regional ingredient on the menu. No: absolutely everything that's served in Dok is made in Israel. It's not about nationalism – the restaurant's ingredients are sourced from Palestinian producers as well as Jewish ones – but rather about a unique sense of place. So, for example, tahini is missing from the menu because all Israeli and Palestinian brands import their sesame seeds, mainly from Ethiopia. The only native sesame that Asaf could find – grown by a hobbyist in the north of the country – turned out to be unsuitable for making tahini. After giving the problem more thought, Asaf realised that he could leave clichéd tahini dishes to Tel Aviv's other restaurants: the purpose of his self-imposed straitjacket – at first glance just a fun gimmick – was to force himself to find creative solutions outside his comfort zone. When the *baladi* ('native') sesame seeds turned out to be unsuitable for tahini, Asaf used them to make ice cream. He produces his own tonic made from self-picked bitter city oranges and mixes it with gin from a micro-distillery in Galilee. The result looks nothing like a normal gin and tonic, but it's the tastiest version I've ever had.

The largely vegetarian menu at Dok is simple yet ingenious. The dishes never contain more than a handful of ingredients, but Asaf continually challenges his guests by serving ostensibly boring vegetables in unusual and delicious ways. This is where I fell head over heels in love with kohlrabi, a tuber that I'd hitherto given nary a second glance. Asaf roasts them whole over the coals, which gives them an intensely earthy flavour that's delicious combined with sheep's cheese and olive oil. A version of this dish was first served at Ha'achim, but to fit Dok's criteria it had to be tweaked: the poppy seeds from the original recipe were replaced by those Israeli sesame seeds; the *hameiri* (a sheep's cheese from Safed), was allowed to stay, but the freshly ground pepper was replaced with finely chopped baladi chillies.

Dok's magical kohlrabi dish alone is worth a trip to Tel Aviv. Try it at home first – with some small concessions – if you don't believe me.

Preheat the oven to its highest setting, ideally 300°C (570°F). Roast the kohlrabi in the centre of the oven for 1–1¼ hours, turning over halfway through cooking. When the skin is completely blackened and the kohlrabi feel soft at the top, remove from the oven and set aside to cool for 5–10 minutes.

When cool enough to handle, peel the charred skin from the kohlrabi using your hands, leaving the skin around the stalk intact.

Just before serving, reheat the kohlrabi in a hot oven (180°C/350°F) for 5 minutes. Plate the kohlrabi and drizzle a generous amount of olive oil over each. Sprinkle with sea salt flakes and garnish with the chilli, thyme, feta and sesame or poppy seeds.

65 g (2¼ oz/¼ cup) tahini with roasted
  garlic (page 282)

2 vine tomatoes, roughly chopped
pinch of salt
handful of hazelnuts
2 large eggplants (aubergines)
sea salt flakes and freshly ground black
  pepper
2 tablespoons pomegranate seeds
2 mint sprigs, leaves coarsely chopped
extra virgin olive oil

ROASTED EGGPLANT WITH TAHINI, HAZELNUTS AND POMEGRANATE SEEDS

Almost every great restaurant in TLV has a version of this dish on its menu – and the inimitable eggplant plays a starring role. Said eggplant is roasted over an open fire until its flesh takes on an irresistibly smoky flavour. After the blackened skin is peeled away and the naked eggplant (you can leave his hat on) is laid elegantly on a plate, a world of possibilities opens up. Just by adding a generous dash of olive oil and some salt and pepper you'll already have a fantastic mezze dish. However, I can't exercise such self-control. I'll admit that the addition of two sauces, pomegranate seeds, hazelnuts and mint seems excessive, but I promise that each ingredient manages to add something to the dish in terms of taste, texture and colour without overpowering the eggplant.

Preheat the oven to 180°C (350°F).

Purée the tomatoes with a pinch of salt using a hand-held blender. Set aside to allow the pectin in the tomatoes to thicken the purée.

Scatter the hazelnuts on a bakingtray and bake for 8–10 minutes, until lightly golden brown. Watch carefully as they will burn easily. Tip the nuts onto a clean tea towel and rub gently in the tea towel to remove the skins.

Blacken the eggplants over the open fire of your gas hob or, if you don't have a gas stove, in the oven under the grill (broiler) (see instructions on page 299). Set aside to cool slightly, then peel off the blackened skin. Leave the stalks on.

Just before serving, preheat the oven to 120°C (250°F). Warm the eggplants on serving plates in the oven for about 5 minutes. Remove from the oven and flatten each eggplant slightly with a fork, then season with sea salt flakes. Criss-cross the eggplants with elegant drizzles of the tahini and tomato purée. Sprinkle with the pomegranate seeds, hazelnuts, mint and freshly ground black pepper, and finish with a drizzle of olive oil.

ROASTED RADISH AND SPRING ONION WITH MACKEREL AND SUMAC

Serves 4

2 teaspoons fennel seeds
2 teaspoons cumin seeds
16 large salad onions (see note in
    introduction), trimmed
30–40 radishes, halved
extra virgin olive oil
pinch of sea salt flakes
1 tablespoon balsamic vinegar
1 whole smoked mackerel, filleted
60 g (2 oz/¼ cup) Greek-style yoghurt
a few pinches of sumac to serve

If I've learned one thing from my time in the kitchens of TLV, it's that many vegetables benefit from doing time in the oven. Take radishes. After a quarter of an hour under a glowing grill, this humble salad vegetable suddenly becomes the main event. Leave the little tails on for aesthetic effect.

For the sake of clarity: there are many varieties of spring onion besides the spindly ones you find in the supermarket. For this recipe I use a larger, more bulbous salad onion. If you can only find bog-standard spring onions, it's not the end of the world. What will affect this dish is the quality of mackerel you can source: seek out the very best on the same day as you plan to cook this dish, and store it outside of the fridge.

Preheat your grill (broiler) to 250°C (480°F). Turn off the oven's fan if it has one.

Grind the fennel and cumin seeds lightly using a mortar and pestle (or skip this step if you don't own one – don't use ground seeds).

Put the onions, radishes, and fennel and cumin seeds into a roasting tray and drizzle with a dash of olive oil. Mix well and roast in the middle of the oven for 20 minutes, or until the vegetables are crisped at the edges and golden brown.

Remove the roasting tin from the oven, season the vegetables with a pinch of salt and drizzle with the balsamic vinegar. Toss well.

Divide the vegetable mixture equally among four plates. Top with chunky flakes of the smoked mackerel. Garnish with dots of the yoghurt, a drizzle of olive oil and a sprinkling of sumac.

12 white asparagus spears, trimmed
    and peeled
simple olive oil for frying
2 tablespoons fresh young thyme sprigs,
    plus extra to garnish
2 green chillies, deseeded and roughly
    chopped
20 g (¾ oz/¼ cup) grated parmesan
juice of ½ lime
extra virgin olive oil
1 pitta
2 teaspoons za'atar
sea salt flakes

CHARGRILLED WHITE ASPARAGUS WITH THYME AND PITTA CROUTONS

You rarely come across white asparagus spears in Israel. I've seen them once or twice at the farmers' market in the old harbour of Tel Aviv, but in nice restaurants, asparagus spears are invariably green. That's a shame, because in the hands of Israeli chefs, white asparagus spears would taste much more exciting than they do in most European restaurants.

To begin with, they would never boil or steam them – firstly because the texture is too wet, and secondly because any garnish with the slightest hint of flavour instantly becomes too dominant. No, in the innovative kitchens of Tel Aviv, white asparagus spears would be oven-roasted at a low temperatures, then finished on the chargrill. They would reach your table sporting beautiful golden-brown stripes, and the flavour imbued by the coals would be more than a match for a spicy sauce. As a finishing touch, Israeli chefs would garnish the dish with a sprinkle of crisp pitta croutons seasoned with za'atar. You wouldn't believe your taste buds.

Preheat the oven to 150°C (300°F). Rub the asparagus spears with the simple olive oil, arrange them in a heavy-based (ideally cast-iron), ovenproof saucepan, and cook in the oven for 25–30 minutes, until they have cooked a little but still retain some bite.

The sauce is a variation on zhug (page 306), the classic Yemeni garnish for sabich and falafel. If your thyme is young enough (those picked straight from the plant are ideal), you can eat the stalks; otherwise, pick the leaves from the thyme and purée them with the chillies, parmesan, lime juice and a glug of the extra virgin olive oil using a hand-held blender. Add more oil as needed until the sauce has the consistency of a thin pesto.

Heat a thick layer of simple olive oil in a heavy-based frying pan. Add the pitta pieces and fry until crisp and pale golden brown. Remove from the pan using a slotted spoon and set aside to drain on paper towel. Sprinkle with the za'atar.

Heat a chargrill pan until smoking hot. Chargrill the asparagus spears for about 1 minute on each side, or until golden-brown stripes have scarred the spears. Arrange the asparagus spears on plates and season with salt. Criss-cross the spears with drizzles of the sauce and garnish with the croutons and thyme sprigs.

BEETROOT CARPACCIO

Serves 4

6 large beetroot (beets)
extra virgin olive oil
2 tablespoons grated fresh horseradish
75 g (2¾ oz) crème fraîche
sea salt flakes

Modern Israeli cuisine owes its success largely to its simplicity. To say that Israeli chefs hate pretentious stacks garnished with foams and edible flowers would be an understatement – they're not even keen on plates. In Eyal Shani's restaurants, for example, plates have been completely abolished, in favour of food served defiantly on sheets of baking paper and cardboard.

It was at Tzfon Abraxas (North Abraxass) that I first got acquainted with Shani's no-frills cooking style. Sitting at the horseshoe-shaped bar I ate dishes containing no more than one main ingredient, which almost sent me to sleep when I read them on the menu, but whose flavours turned out to be sensational. Eyal Shani taught me to taste everyday vegetables such as cauliflower, green beans and beetroot in a new way.

You have to be brave to pull this off: after all, your guests are coming to your restaurant with high expectations, and on the face of it, a piece of cardboard topped with thinly sliced beetroot is not going to cut it. But this is no cheap gimmick. Eyal Shani is obsessed with the essential flavours of his ingredients; for him, everything else – including his own fame – is just a distraction from the food.

Shani is fortunate to have fantastic produce from his native soil at his disposal, those of us wanting to imitate his dishes outside of Israel are not always so blessed. Many of the vegetables we buy are grown in greenhouses or imported, and they don't hold a candle to crops that have ripened under the blazing Israeli sun. Where I live in the Netherlands, beetroot are a pleasant exception.

I've tweaked this recipe a little by mixing some grated horseradish through the crème fraîche; personally, I find the combination of beetroot and horseradish irresistible. If you can't get fresh horseradish, just leave it out. After all, less is more.

Set the oven to its highest setting, ideally 300°C (570°F). Rub the beetroot with the oil, place them onto a baking tray and roast for 1¼–2 hours, until the skin is completely blackened (winter beetroot need a little longer). Turn the beetroot over halfway through cooking.

Meanwhile, blend the grated horseradish and crème fraîche to a smooth cream using a hand-held blender. Chill until needed.

When the beetroot are cooked, remove from the oven and set aside to cool to room temperature. Then carefully peel away most of the charred skin. Cut the beetroot into wafer-thin slices using a mandoline.

To serve, scrunch a sheet of baking paper into a ball, then spread it out onto a chopping board. Arrange the sliced beetroot on the paper. Season with the salt and a drizzle of the olive oil, and dollops of the horseradish cream.

COMFORT FOOD, ASHKENAZI STYLE

There are few pieces of meat that provoke as much disgust as the tongue of a cow. Just the idea of it makes people put their foot down; nine times out of ten, Dutch people will come out with the same half-baked argument: 'I don't eat anything that's already been in another's mouth.' More fool them, because tongue is one of the most divine flavours you'll find. Its virtues are twofold: it's at once full of flavour and has a buttery yet firm texture.

Because Jewish food laws prohibit the consumption of tender fillets from the cow's haunch (see page 191), tongue emerged as a popular alternative to steak – a truly classic Ashkenazi dish is tongue served with sweet-and-sour sauce.

In Israel, however, tongue was not a staple of the diet. At first, all meat was scarce; besides, between the wars, people were just too busy building their young country. Eating and drinking were a necessary evil that shouldn't take up too much time. The time-consuming preparation of tongue – two days brining plus a few hours bubbling on the stove – was a luxury that no one could permit themselves.

Those hectic pioneering years are long gone and today, Israelis are among the most prolific consumers of meat in the world. However, tongue has still taken quite some time to make its comeback. In restaurants, Sephardic cuisine has gained the upper hand and Ashkenazi showpieces such as gefilte fish, chopped liver and tongue are relegated to luxury beach resorts, where they're ordered on Shabbat by Jewish tourists hankering for their traditional comfort food. In recent years, more and more young chefs have been going against the grain and – inspired by the slow-food movement, with its emphasis on traditional cuisine – have started reintroducing experimental versions of the food of their eastern-European ancestors, particularly tongue. Take Jonathan Borowitz's trendy restaurant, M25, where the beef tongue sits in brine for two full weeks. Borowitz serves it sliced, with mustard and *chrain* (horseradish sauce) – exactly like his Lithuanian grandmother used to.

SMOKED BEEF TONGUE WITH BEETROOT AND QUAIL EGGS

Tongue struggles with an old-fashioned image and its recent star turn on a handful of menus in trendy Tel Aviv restaurants has done little to change this preconception. The preparation and presentation of tongue has remained unchanged for generations: it's simmered in broth, then sliced and served with a sweet-sour sauce made from cooked fruit. The only change has been semantic: when young chefs put this vintage classic on their menu, it's no longer 'old-fashioned', but 'retro'. There's nothing wrong with this, except that retro dishes don't tend to have a long shelf life.

This is my twist on that good old-fashioned recipe for tongue: the sophisticated, intensely meaty flavour of the tongue combines perfectly with the earthy, sweet character of the beetroot and the fresh crunch of radish sprouts. I also replaced the mighty sweet-and-sour sauce with a more delicate vinaigrette made with fresh thyme. The result? I succeeded in converting many sceptics to tongue (tip: only reveal the true identity of the meat after the person eating has complimented you on it).

This recipe takes quite some time to prepare if you don't know any butchers who sell tongue ready brined (mine brines the tongue for two days and smokes it for half a day). You may struggle to find such a butcher – due to the perfect storm of strict environmental legislation, complaining neighbours and low demand for organ meat, most tongue meat now ends up in the meat grinder.

Once you've sourced a pre-pickled and smoked beef tongue, preparing this dish is suddenly a piece of cake. In fact, this recipe produces two further delicious meals: you can use the stock to make smoky tomato soup with meatballs (page 192) and the left-over meat as the basis of a fantastic Hussar's salad (a Dutch version of Russian salad, page 251).

Serves 4

STOCK
1 large leek, cut into large pieces
1 × 1.5 kg–2 kg (3 lb 5 oz–4 lb 6½ oz) brined, smoked beef tongue
1 celery, cut into large pieces (leaves reserved)
1 large carrot, cut into large pieces
2 onions, halved
1 marrow bone
1 calf's knuckle
6 garlic cloves
4 bay leaves
6 thyme sprigs
10 black peppercorns
1 tablespoon salt (if your tongue is not kosher)

VINAIGRETTE
50 ml (1¾ fl oz) white wine vinegar
½ teaspoon dijon mustard
150 ml (5 fl oz) extra virgin olive oil
1 shallot, finely chopped
1 tablespoon fresh young thyme, finely chopped
salt and freshly ground black pepper
10 quail eggs
2 ready-cooked, ready-peeled beetroot (beets)
30 g (1 oz/½ cup) radish sprouts

For the stock, arrange the leek pieces in a layer at the bottom of a large, heavy-based saucepan and lay the beef tongue on top. Add the remaining broth ingredients to the pan, packing them down as tightly as possible. Add enough water to just cover the ingredients and bring to the boil. Turn the heat down to its lowest setting and simmer the stock gently. A 1.5 kg (3 lb 5 oz) tongue will need to be cooked for about 2 hours; add 1 hour for every extra 500 g (1 lb 2 oz). The tongue is tender when the membrane at the tip comes away easily. (Reserve the broth for use in the smoky tomato soup recipe; page 192.)

Recipe continues overleaf

Continued from previous page

Remove the cooked tongue from the stock using a slotted spoon. Run it under cold water until still warm but cool enough to handle, then peel away the outer membrane of the tongue. Seal the peeled tongue in a zip-lock bag so that it cools completely without drying out.

For the vinaigrette, whisk the vinegar and mustard in a bowl until well combined gradually add the oil in a thin stream, whisking continuously, until the vinaigrette thickens and emulsifies. Whisk in the shallot and thyme and season with salt and freshly ground black pepper. You will have more vinaigrette than you need for this recipe, but you can use left-over vinaigrette in my Hussar's salad (page 251).

Just before serving, soft-boil the quail eggs (this will take 2–3 minutes), then drain and run under cold water until cool enough to handle. Peel carefully.

Cut the beetroot into wafer-thin slices using a mandoline. Arrange the beetroot slices in concentric circles on four plates. Cut long thin slices from the best-looking side of the cooked tongue and lay 2–3 slices per person on top of the beetroot. Garnish each plate with the radish sprouts and halved quail eggs. Drizzle over a little of the vinaigrette.

3 eggs
salt and freshly ground black pepper
1 tablespoon finely chopped chives
1 tablespoon finely chopped flat-leaf
    (Italian) parsley
1 tablespoon finely chopped fresh
    young thyme
1 tablespoon dijon mustard
1 tablespoon schmaltz (page 308) or
    olive oil
65 g (2¼ oz) veal ham (not too lean),
    coarsely chopped
2 tablespoons chopped cress

HERB OMELETTE WITH VEAL HAM AND CRESS

Because I eat kosher at home, every meal starts with the choice between either dairy or meat (or neither – that is, of course, also allowed). For breakfast that choice is easy to make, because who doesn't want to start the day with butter, cheese and eggs? At that time of day, when my stomach is empty and my taste buds are only half awake, meat is the last thing I need.

There's one exception to this rule: the hangover breakfast. When I go to bed drunk, I wake up like a bloodthirsty carnivore. I don't know whether or not animal fat helps me to sober up, but after a drink-soaked evening, my body craves meat – and I listen to it. If I don't find any left-over shawarma or half-eaten chicken in the refrigerator, I tend to make this omelette. To keep it kosher I fry it in schmaltz (page 308), but if you want to use butter (and pork ham, for that matter), be my guest.

Whisk the eggs in a bowl and season with a pinch of salt and freshly ground black pepper. Whisk in the chives, parsley, thyme and mustard. Don't whisk for too long, as you will knock the air out of your eggs.

Heat the fat in a frying pan over medium heat. Pour in the egg mixture. Move the pan so that the still-liquid egg is evenly distributed inside the omelette, then turn down the heat to its lowest setting and let the omelette cook slowly.

Just before the omelette is completely cooked through, cover half of it with the veal ham and cress and fold the other side over the filling using a spatula. Slide the omelette onto a plate and eat with toast, a glass of water and paracetamol.

Tzfon Abraxas

THE SECRET OF FLORENTIN

'Why don't you start a restaurant?' people ask me with some regularity. My answer is always the same: 'Because if you really love cooking, you shouldn't become a chef.'

'Why don't you start a restaurant?' people ask me with some regularity. My answer is always the same: 'Because if you really love cooking, you shouldn't become a chef.' I would find it terrible to spend night after night mechanically throwing together the same dishes in a brightly lit kitchen, in the hope that staff will deliver compliments from tables one through 25. Working in the hospitality industry is like starting a B&B in your favourite holiday destination: it sounds like a dream come true, an eternal holiday, and so on – but in reality it's back-breaking work and doomed to fail. That's why I prefer cooking at home for self-selected guests. Then I can join them at the table and enjoy their lip-smacking.

But now I've started to doubt my reasoning – and it's all down to a new restaurant in Tel Aviv that I tried recently, which has a brilliant concept. In Florentin, the last remaining neighbourhood yet to fall victim to project developers, television chef Barak Yehezkeli has started a restaurant that is open only one evening per week. It's called Burek and it's totally awesome.

Every Wednesday evening, groups of people wander around the narrow, graffiti-plastered alleyways of this small hipster neighbourhood, anxiously searching for Burek. It's no use asking local residents, because the location is the best kept secret in the city. Once you find it, you're welcomed by the red-haired chef himself, who hands you an arak cocktail. From the balcony, a DJ fills the dining room with sultry jazz beats. In the middle of the room, which has space for just a handful of tables, is the open kitchen. The chefs clustered around this cooking island preparing your starter are professionals who work in other kitchens during the rest of the week. Everyone here eats the same dishes, but special dietary requirements are dealt with generously.

Think Jackson Pollock reincarnated as a confectioner. Everyone is given a dessert spoon and told to dig in. No one thinks about germs. This is Tel Aviv.

Co-owner Jonathan, who sports the same shade of red hair as Barak but in the style of Beaker from *The Muppet Show*, takes care of the layout of the dining room. There is one table for two that caters to loved-up couples; the rest of the tables are communal. An evening at Burek is like going to a dinner party of a friend who has also invited some people you don't know. The first course, a selection of vegetables, is for the whole table. Soon the table will order its first joint bottle of wine and Facebook friendships will be sealed. Chef Yehezkeli occasionally proposes a *l'chaim* (toast) and encourages his guests to come and nose around in the kitchen.

Barak introduces each course with a short explanation. He tells guests that he spends Tuesdays alternately in the north or the south of the country, hunting for special ingredients from the small-scale farmers and growers there that he can use in his dishes. He does the rest of his grocery shopping for the restaurant at the Wednesday-morning market.

When it's time for dessert, everyone has to gather round the cooking island. It's been covered with baking paper by Barak and his men, who – like accomplished live-action painters – proceed to cover the paper with splats of chocolate, daubs of crème fraîche, cherries and pears in white wine, crème brûlée, caramelised bananas, millefeuille bites and crunchy almond waffles. Think Jackson Pollock reincarnated as a confectioner. Everyone is given a dessert spoon and told to dig in. No one thinks about germs. This is Tel Aviv.

Burek is my favourite restaurant in Tel Aviv. That's in part due to the great food, but also because everyone always has a lot of fun there – the guests, sure, but the chefs too. Their cooking is a huge part of the experience, and the set-up allows the chefs to become guests at their own party. Because the restaurant is only open one day per week, the ingredients are never anything but market-fresh, and the chefs never get bored. It's not a restaurant concept to get rich from – but luckily Barak earns enough money from his television work and by renting out the restaurant space for private parties.

Who knows, maybe I will start my own restaurant after all.

ROASTED EGGPLANT WITH APPLE, HAZELNUTS AND SILAN

Serves 6

4 tablespoons tahini (page 282)

4 eggplants (aubergines)
1 granny smith (or similar tart, green apple), peeled, cored and chopped into small pieces
1 teaspoon ground cumin
½ teaspoon ground cinnamon
100 g (3½ oz/¾ cup) hazelnuts
sea salt flakes
1 red chilli, deseeded and thinly sliced
extra virgin olive oil
silan or date syrup
6 pinches of sumac

Eggplant and apple are certainly not a classic combination, but these two fruits – one typically Israeli, the other very Dutch – actually work really well together. I made this dish for an Israeli chef who had allowed me to work an afternoon shift in his restaurant. He looked rather doubtful when I asked him for the ingredients, but when he tasted the finished dish, his scepticism melted away like snow in the sun. In fact, he demanded that the entire kitchen brigade come and taste it. I was only allowed to leave once I had written down the recipe.

Blacken the eggplants over the flame of your gas hob, or if you do not have a gas stove, under the grill (broiler) of the oven (see instructions on page 299). Set the eggplants aside to cool slightly, then peel off the blackened skin.

Mix the apple with the spices in a bowl and set aside. Toast the hazelnuts in a dry frying pan over medium–high heat until they are scorched golden brown. Coarsely chop the nuts and set aside.

Just before serving, preheat the oven to 120°C (250°F), transfer the eggplants and hazelnuts to a roasting tray and warm through for 4–5 minutes. Chop the eggplants coarsely and season with sea salt flakes. Add the spiced apple and chilli to the roasting tray and toss to combine.

To serve, divide the eggplant mixture equally among six plates. Drizzle generously with olive oil.

Criss-cross the eggplant mixture with drizzles of tahini and silan, then finish with a pinch of sumac.

ARAK ATTACK

Every country on the Mediterranean coast has developed its own beloved liqueur from anise. The Greeks have ouzo, the French pastis, the Italians sambuca, the Turks raki – and the Israelis? They have arak. I've never really understood why anise is the common denominator in the Mediterranean liquor cabinet. Why on earth would you want an alcoholic drink that tastes like licorice?

Although I want to like everything, I never really bothered to get a taste for arak. It was just a fuddy-duddy liqueur enjoyed mainly by Sephardic pensioners and Christian Arabs. Moreover, it was difficult to come by: although arak is produced throughout the Arab world, the Muslim owners of the Middle Eastern shops in my area don't sell alcohol.

In recent years, arak has made a surprise comeback. This is partly due to the economic crisis: arak is a cheap way to have a drink. The rehabilitation of Sephardic cuisine – once held in contempt, now the subject of an almost evangelical devotion – has also played a role: Sephardic dishes pepper trendy menus, Sephardic music sets the tone in the dining room – and arak is increasingly displacing whisky and vodka in people's shot glasses. And if there's a bottle of arak going round, you don't want to be the only party pooper not joining in with the toast.

After a while I started to love arak. Initially, it was because I associated the taste with the exuberance of Tel Aviv's nightlife. Then, when drinking on the beach and in cocktail bars, I started choosing cocktails made with arak.

Wrapped up in socks and trouser legs I started to take bottles of arak back home to Amsterdam every time I left Tel Aviv. That's no longer necessary, since in my home city of Amsterdam, a Moroccan Jew called Jack Tordjman now distils his own aniseed liqueur, which he has christened 'arakino', and which (I swear) tastes better than most Israeli versions. I've been experimenting with arakino and have come up with three summery cocktails that will bring a Tel Avivian flavour to proceedings. If you can't find arak (or, indeed, arakino) where you live, use another aniseed liqueur such as ouzo.

Serves 4

1 small seedless watermelon
200 ml (7 fl oz) arak (40% abv)
juice of 1 lime, plus 1 whole lime
    to garnish
3 tablespoons maple syrup
20 ice cubes
4 mint sprigs

Cut open the watermelon and cut 40 small cubes from it. Put the watermelon cubes into the smallest container you can fit them into. Pour over the arak and set aside to steep, then transfer to the freezer for at least 1 hour.

Purée the remaining watermelon flesh using a hand-held blender. Pour 600 ml (20½ fl oz) of the watermelon juice into a jug and add the lime juice and maple syrup. Cover and chill in the refrigerator.

Just before serving, remove the watermelon cubes from the freezer and drain them through a fine-mesh sieve, reserving the arak in a measuring jug. Top up the drained arak to 200 ml (7 fl oz) using arak from the bottle. Add this mixture to the jug of watermelon juice and stir to combine.

Gather the ice cubes in a clean tea towel and crush with a rolling pin. Spoon the crushed ice into the bottom of four cocktail glasses. Divide the frozen watermelon cubes equally among the glasses, then top up with the watermelon juice. Quarter the remaining lime and garnish each glass with a mint sprig and lime wedge. Serve with a teaspoon and a straw.

From left to right: Arak attack, Arak with grapefruit and grenadine, and 'Apple juice'

ARAK WITH GRAPEFRUIT AND GRENADINE

On the beaches of Tel Aviv, the combination of arak and grapefruit juice is as quintessential as gin and tonic or rum and cola. If you can get your hands on excellent-quality fresh grapefruit juice from the supermarket, it will save you the trouble of squeezing all those grapefruit.

Serves 4

600 ml (20¼ fl oz) pink-grapefruit juice
200 ml (7 fl oz) arak (40% abv)
juice of 1 lime
25 ml (1 fl oz) grenadine
   (pomegranate cordial)
20 ice cubes
4 pink grapefruit wedges, to serve
4 mint sprigs

Mix the pink-grapefruit juice, arak, lime juice and grenadine in a jug. (Chill in the refrigerator for as long as possible before serving.) Gather the ice cubes in a clean tea towel and crush with a rolling pin. Divide the crushed ice equally among four cocktail glasses. Fill the glasses with the pink-grapefruit mixture. Float a pink-grapefruit wedge in each cocktail, and garnish each glass with a mint sprig. Serve with a straw and a muddler.

See photo on page 155.

'ARAPPLE JUICE'

At Miznon, Eyal Shani's peerless pitta-based snack bar, I drank arak mixed with apple juice for the first time. It was the best long drink I could have wished for when the heat was 38 (100) degrees in the shade.

Serves 4

20 ice cubes
200 ml (7 fl oz) arak (40% abv)
600 ml (20½ fl oz) organic cloudy
   apple juice
200 ml (7 fl oz) cold water
20 wafer-thin lime slices
4 mint sprigs

Gather the ice cubes in a clean tea towel and crush with a rolling pin. Divide equally among four highball glasses. Pour 50 ml (1¾ fl oz) of the arak, then 50 ml (1¾ fl oz) of the apple juice, then 50 ml (1¾ fl oz) of the water into each glass. Stir well. Slide a stack of 5 lime slices into each glass and insert a mint sprig between them.

ELI'S MSABBAHA

Serves 4

8 tablespoons caramelised onions
   (page 287)
4 laffa (page 300) to serve

60 g (2 oz/¼ cup) labneh or Greek-
   style yoghurt
60 g (2 oz/¼ cup) sour cream
salt and freshly ground black pepper
40 g (1½ oz/¼ cup) pine nuts
350 g (12½ oz/1¾ cups) tinned chickpeas
1 teaspoon coriander seeds
1 teaspoon cumin seeds
extra virgin olive oil
4 flat-leaf (Italian) parsley sprigs,
   coarsely chopped

'Better than hummus!' exclaims Eli Shtein, throwing modesty aside as he takes a lick of his own sauce. The young chef has just prepared his contribution to my cookbook in the small kitchen of his restaurant, Ramesses: fish tabouleh with labneh cream and caramelised onion (page 164).

By his twenties, Eli, an emigrant from the Ukraine, had already built up an impressive career, heading up kitchens in top restaurants such as Herbert Samuel, Taizu and Toto – where he was younger than the youngest dishwasher. For some time he has had his own open-air restaurant, on the narrow streets of Jaffa.

Eli predicts a great future for his sauce: according to him, all that's missing is a large-scale producer to put it onto the market. Putting his money where his mouth is, he prepares me his msabbaha, an alternative for the traditionally run-of-the-mill coarse hummus, served lukewarm. With the bottom of his spoon, Eli then spreads his sauce over a plate and spoons warm chickpeas on top. We dig in, and there's no comparison: using laffa, we scrape the plate clean. When Eli finds a manufacturer for his sauce, I'm buying shares.

Blend the caramelised onions, labneh and sour cream to a smooth purée using a hand-held blender. Season with salt and freshly ground black pepper.

Toast the pine nuts in a dry frying pan until golden brown – keep your eye on them as they will burn quickly. Tip the chickpeas, and the chickpea water from the tin, into a separate saucepan. Grind the coriander and cumin seeds using a mortar and pestle.

Divide the onion mixture among four small plates and spread thinly with the bottom of a spoon. Spoon the warm chickpeas over the onion mixture, sprinkle with the ground coriander and cumin, and drizzle with a generous splash of olive oil. Garnish with the toasted pine nuts and the parsley.

Serve Eli's msabbaha with warm laffa.

Serves 4

FISH TABOULEH

2 tablespoons fine bulgur (burghul)
2 tablespoons pine nuts
1 teaspoon coriander seeds
1 teaspoon cumin seeds
4 × 300 g (10½ oz) super-fresh red snapper fillets
1 small onion, finely chopped
½ bunch flat-leaf (Italian) parsley, leaves
    and stalks chopped
½ lemon
1–2 tablespoons balsamic vinegar
extra virgin olive oil
salt and freshly ground black pepper

CREAM

80 g (2¾ oz/¼ cup) caramelised onions (page 287)
2 tablespoons labneh or Greek-style yoghurt
2 tablespoons sour cream

GARNISH

pinch of cayenne pepper
handful of pea shoots

For the fish tabouleh, soak the bulgur in lukewarm water for 30 minutes. Meanwhile, make the cream. Purée the caramelised onions, labneh and sour cream as smooth as possible using a hand-held blender. Season the mixture with salt and freshly ground black pepper.

When the bulgur has soaked, drain the grains through a fine-mesh sieve and use a piece of paper towel to squeeze out as much water as possible.

Toast the pine nuts in a dry frying pan until golden brown – keep your eye on them as they will burn quickly. Set aside to cool, then chop roughly. Grind the coriander and cumin seeds using a mortar and pestle.

Moisten a razor-sharp kitchen knife and slice the fish into small cubes. Transfer to a bowl and add the bulgur, pine nuts, ground spices, onion and parsley. Squeeze over the lemon juice, then drizzle with the balsamic vinegar and a generous splash of olive oil. Work all of the ingredients together and season with salt and pepper.

Spread a spoonful of the cream artfully onto each plate. Heap some of the fish tabouleh on top. Drizzle again with olive oil and garnish with a pinch of cayenne pepper and the pea shoots.

FISH TABOULEH WITH LABNEH CREAM AND CARAMELISED ONION

Only the guests who use the toilet get to see the inside of Jaffa's coolest restaurant, because all of the tables at Ramesses are right in the middle of the street outside. At night, the surroundings are enchanting: the weathered stone houses of the old Arab district are lit up with a yellow glow, making them stand out against the dark sky. During the day, this neighbourhood is the domain of flea-market stallholders, artisans and artists – and the bargain hunters who come to scour their wares for something they didn't know they wanted in the first place.

I look at my phone: it's 2am. In a couple of hours the doors of the various storage units will be rolled open and the curios, furniture and artworks inside will be dragged out again for display. For the time being, however, the streets belong to the young crowds out on the town, all of whom give the impression that the night is still young.

While my photographer Vincent tries to capture the scene, I chat with a newly arrived couple who are too tipsy to concentrate on the menu. I recommend the fantastic dish that chef Eli Shtein had prepared for me earlier that afternoon in the kitchen across the street – on the menu it's under the heading 'Chopping board & knife'. The young chef has a penchant for dishes that come to the plate with minimal preparation.

All around me, people are eating and drinking with gusto. The DJ mixes the guests' voices with exotic sounds that I can't define as Arabic or Sephardic. Just as Vincent calls to me that he's ready to go, a waitress brings the couple their starter: fish tabouleh with labneh cream and caramelised onion. As we pass their table, they give us the thumbs up. *'Beteavon!'* ('Enjoy your meal!') I call back.

Serves 4

1 × quantity tahini (page 282)
1 × quantity pitta chips (crisps) (page 292)

PICKLED ONIONS
200 ml (7 fl oz) red wine vinegar
40 g (1½ oz) granulated sugar
1 chilli, sliced into thin rings
2 red onions, roughly chopped

SINIYA
4 vine tomatoes, quartered
simple olive oil
3 teaspoons za'atar
1 large eggplant (aubergine), cut into
    2 cm (¾in) slices
sea salt flakes
sunflower or peanut oil for frying
1 large white onion, finely chopped
2 garlic cloves, crushed
250 g (9 oz) minced (ground) lamb
250 g (9 oz) minced (ground) beef
1 teaspoon ground cumin
½ teaspoon ground cinnamon
2 tablespoons pine nuts, toasted
salt and freshly ground black pepper

D & A'S SINIYA

Adi came to the Netherlands in her thirties. Her intention was to take a six-month break to recover from the hectic pace of life in Israel. Twelve years on, Adi is still in Amsterdam, where she runs D & A Hummus Bistro, a little slice of Tel Aviv in the heart of the Jordaan neighbourhood. Here you can get stuck into comforting hummus dishes and other classics, from shakshuka to falafel to chraime.

When Adi lost her job a few years ago and struggled to find a new one, she decided to start her own business. Since she regularly made hummus at home and her father had once run a hummus bar in Tel Aviv, she decided pretty quickly to open a restaurant. Ana, an acquaintance from the school run, had experience as a chef. Being of Indian descent, Ana didn't know anything about Israeli cuisine, but when Adi asked her to become her chef, she agreed. Adi's parents came to Amsterdam to give Ana a crash course in Israeli cooking – for two weeks they cooked family recipes toegether in Adi's apartment, working from early in the morning until late at night. As a result, Ana now makes the best hummus in the city.

As soon as my homesickness for Tel Aviv starts to rear its head, I jump on my bike and head to D & A. Usually, I order the siniya. Strictly speaking, this Palestinian dish is a casserole topped with a thick layer of tahini, but in Ana's hands it becomes a delicious stir-fry dish containing two types of minced meat, fried eggplant, crisp pitta chips and a generous dollop of tahini. After a plate of siniya, washed down with an arak and grapefruit juice, I'm back in business.

First, make the pickled onions. Pour 400 ml (13¼ fl oz) of water into a saucepan. Add the vinegar, sugar and chilli and bring to the boil, stirring until the sugar has dissolved. Transfer the liquid to a large bowl, add the red onions and set aside for 1¼ hours to marinate. Drain the onions and set aside.

For the siniya, preheat the oven to 250°C (480°F). Place the tomatoes onto a roasting tray, drizzle with the simple olive oil and sprinkle with 1 teaspoon of the za'atar. Roast in the oven for 15 minutes, or until the tomatoes start to colour. Set aside to cool.

Sprinkle the eggplant slices with sea salt and set aside for 20 minutes. Heat a thick layer of the oil in a large, heavy-based frying pan to 180°C (350°F), or until a breadcrumb immediately turns golden brown when dropped into it. Dry the eggplant slices with paper towel and fry on both sides until golden brown all over. Set aside to drain on paper towel.

Heat a generous splash of the simple olive oil in a frying pan over low heat. Add the white onion and garlic and fry until softened. Increase the heat and add all of the meat, the remaining 2 teaspoons of za'atar, and the ground cumin and cinnamon. Stir-fry, breaking up any clumps of minced meat, until the meat is just cooked through. Add the pine nuts and season with salt and freshly ground black pepper.

Divide the aubergines and tomatoes among four plates. Spoon the meat mixture on top, and a large tablespoon of tahini on top of that. Garnish with the pickled red onion and serve with the pitta chips.

DUCK TAGINE

No disrespect to the noble chicken, but there's a tastier bird in the poultry aisle. With that in mind, it's a complete mystery to me why more people don't serve duck more often. Is Walt Disney to blame? Or does it have something to do with the ducks that we see swimming in the pond in our local park – can't we bring ourselves to eat the feathered friends who gobble up our stale bread so gratefully? The only valid explanation that I can think of for our meagre duck consumption is that duck is more expensive than chicken. But that's because demand for duck meat is so much lower.

The beauty of duck is that it combines all the environmental and (supposed) health benefits of poultry with the red, flavourful meat that we associate with beef or lamb. Preparing it might seem like a challenge, especially if we're talking about a hefty two-kilo bird. But thanks to its thick layer of fatty skin, duck dries out less quickly than chicken, making it perfect for use in a tagine. A tagine is a Moroccan cooking utensil whose lid is shaped like a pointed hat. It slowly steams the food inside, meaning that everything you put into it (meat, fish, vegetables) comes out deliciously tender. You can't really go wrong with a tagine. That's why they're a failsafe dish to cook for a large group – especially on a Friday evening, as Shabbat approaches. With a tagine, all the work is done well in advance of your guests arriving, and even if the food is ready before anyone arrives, it's no problem – simply sit it in a just-warm oven until you're ready to serve. What's more, the beautiful tagine pot can be brought straight to the table. Make sure you get everyone's attention before you lift off the pointed hat.

Serves 6

2 tablespoons TLV spice mix
   (page 288) or ras el hanout/baharat

olive oil
1.5–2 kg (3 lb 5 oz–4 lb 6 oz) duck, jointed
salt and freshly ground black pepper
70 g (2½ oz) tomato paste
   (concentrated purée)
8 shallots, halved
4 garlic cloves, sliced
grated zest of 1 lemon
2 large vine tomatoes, chopped
125 g (4½ oz/1 cup) pitted green olives
3 bay leaves
100–200 ml (3½–7 fl oz) chicken stock
100 g (3½ oz/⅔ cup) blanched almonds,
   halved

Heat a dash of the oil in a 35 cm (14 in) tagine over high heat. Add the duck pieces, skin-side down, and fry in batches, until the skin is golden brown and the fat has melted. Remove from the tagine pot and season with salt and freshly ground black pepper. Once cool enough to handle, smear with the tomato paste.

Fry the shallots, garlic and TLV spice in the fat in the tagine pot for 1–2 minutes. Return the duck pieces to the pot, skin-side up, and sprinkle with the lemon zest. Stir in the tomatoes, olives and bay leaves, then pour over about 100 ml (3½ fl oz) of the stock.

Bring the mixture to a simmer, then reduce the heat to its lowest setting (use a heat diffuser if you have one). Cover the tagine with its lid, and cook for 1½ hours. Check every so often that the tagine isn't drying out, topping up with stock as needed.

Dry-fry the almonds in a frying pan until golden brown and set aside to cool. Sprinkle the duck tagine with the almonds and serve with couscous.

1 × quantity pitta chips (crisps)
    (page 292)
1 × quantity matbukha
    (page 304)

4 ripe avocados, halved, skin
    and stones removed
olive oil
salt and freshly ground black
    pepper
1 lime, cut into wedges

Heat a chargrill pan over high
heat until smoking hot.

Drizzle the cut sides of the
avocados with the oil. Grill
the avocados, cut-sides
down, for about 1 minute,
until golden-brown chargrill
stripes appear. Season with
salt and freshly ground black
pepper, then drizzle with a
little more olive oil.

Serve the grilled avocado
with a lime wedge, some
pitta chips and a small dish
of matbukha.

GRILLED AVOCADO WITH MATBUKHA

More and more these days, we eat with our eyes. It's down to the Instagram culture – tens of thousands of food snapshots, tagged with the dubious recommendations #foodporn and #foodgasm, clamour for attention on the platform every day. Pixels can't be tasted, so the deliciousness of the dish in question is judged on appearance alone. Most comfort food – despite being delicious – doesn't get a look-in, due to the fact that it's usually brown and sludgy. Anyone who cooks with flavour in mind asks themself: are there enough sweet/sour/salty/bitter flavours in my dish? Whereas anyone cooking with visual impact in mind asks themself: is there enough lilac, turquoise and ochre on the plate? Does it need a flash of red? Bring on the pomegranate seeds!

This wouldn't be such a big deal if the phenomenon hadn't infected the entire catering industry. Now, all chefs are aware of the need to produce dishes that are not only delicious but also photogenic, knowing that before their customers pick up their fork, they will first grab their mobile phone and take a picture. And the more approval those pictures receive on social media, the more potential new guests the restaurant will attract. This has resulted in extreme cases of Instagram-baiting – at one Amsterdam restaurant, for example, every dish on the menu contains avocado. For me, such a concept is an abomination: even if it were white truffle I wouldn't want to eat it three courses in a row, however much I might like the ingredient itself. But for me, the worst thing is how the avocados are modelled into fancy pieces of art. Meticulously decorated avocado roses might look ruggedly handsome, but more than anything, they demonstrate that taste is only being regarded as secondary.

Although the Instagram craze has reached TLV, an avocado-themed restaurant would be unthinkable here. The average Israeli consumes five kilos of avocados per year – more than twice as many as people in western Europe. Only Mexicans eat more. In addition, Israel exports about six percent of the total world supply of avocados – and that's without taking into account production for consumption at home, which is about 40 percent of the harvest. These avocados are only picked when fully ripe – they're so creamy and flavourful that you don't have to do much with them when cooking.

Elsewhere we often have to make do with third-rate avocados, but consumption continues to rise regardless. Yet the way we fetishise avocados proves that we do not yet fully appreciate their true flavour. If we did, we would simply mash them, like the Mexicans do, or chargrill them, like at Ha'achim in Tel Aviv. It is, of course, a matter of taste, I find avocados decorated with smoky grill stripes much more appealing than ingeniously crafted avocado roses and in any case, much more delicious.

SEPHARDIC FISH

For Shabbat, my mother would lay on a spread. On Friday evenings we sat with the whole family around a table laden with Ashkenazi classics: chopped liver, chicken soup and, sometimes, gefilte fish. Although I, unlike my father, ate pretty much everything, as the years went by, my dislike for those slimy fish balls grew and grew.

Although my mother is of Sephardic origin (her ancestors fled the Spanish Inquisition and settled in Amsterdam in the 17th century), I grew up eating the Ashkenazi dishes of my father's family. Not that my dad did the cooking (according to family folklore, he once tried to fry an egg in vinegar). Instead, using her excellent cooking skills, my mother adapted to the unadventurous tastes of her spouse. On weekdays we would eat one-pot Dutch dishes – with the exception of sauerkraut, carbonade and all stews, because the master of the household didn't like them. In fact, he often ate alone, since by the time he came home from work, my brother and I were already in bed.

For Shabbat, my mother would lay on a spread. On Friday evenings, we would sit with the whole family around a table laden with Ashkenazi classics: chopped liver, chicken soup and, sometimes, gefilte fish. Although I, unlike my father, ate pretty much everything, as the years went by, my dislike for those slimy fish balls grew and grew. Out of respect for all my mother's hard work I would still eat them, preferably buried under a hefty layer of chrain (sweet-sharp horseradish sauce, see page 305). There was nothing wrong with the way she cooked them, there's just not much to say about boiled, sweetened freshwater fish. The death blow came a few years ago: when filming my television series, we had to do about ten takes of me taking a bite of gefilte fish. I haven't eaten it since.

Apart from fish cakes and some cold fish dishes (herring salad, bagels with lox and cream cheese), fish dishes are rather thin on the ground in traditional Jewish cuisine. At least, that's what I grew up thinking, since due to my Ashkenazi upbringing I had never heard of chraime, the Sephardic answer to gefilte fish. I encountered it for the first time in Tel Aviv a few years ago, at Gedera 26, a street-food stall at the edge of the Carmel Market. After the waitress explained to me that chraime had nothing to do with chrain (and my companions had expressed their amazement about my lack of knowledge of Jewish cuisine), I cautiously ordered chraime for the first time. It was love at first bite.

Along with shakshuka and matbukha, chraime is the most important contribution of North African Jews to Israeli cuisine. Matbukha is a spicy sauce made by cooking tomatoes and red capsicums (bell peppers) with garlic and paprika. If you poach eggs into the sauce, you've got shakshuka. If you replace the eggs with fish, it's called chraime.

I still can't work out how I didn't discover chraime earlier. It is offered on the menu in Israeli restaurants as often as pizzas are in pizzerias. And maybe it was just my imagination, but every time I ordered chraime from then on, it tasted even better. The chraime at North Abraxass was better than the one from Gedera 26, and that was beaten by an even better version at Romano. The fact that they could all taste so different was remarkable in itself, since the recipe has so few ingredients to play with.

This is the paradox of classics such as hummus, pesto, pizza margherita and now also chraime: the fewer the ingredients, the easier it is to ruin the dish. Don't let that put you off. I think even my culinarily challenged father would be able to make a success out of my chraime recipe. Actually, probably not. But you get the picture.

The secret lies in sourcing the right ingredients. After a bit of trial and error, the same thing happened to me at home as in Tel Aviv: my second chraime was better than my first, and my fourth or fifth attempts surpassed that of Romano.

I still can't work out how I didn't discover chraime earlier. It is offered on the menu in Israeli restaurants as often as pizzas are in pizzerias.

BONELESS CHRAIME

Serves 4

65 g (2¼ oz/¼ cup) tahini (page 282)

4 red capsicums (bell peppers), cut into
    large pieces
olive oil for frying
3 red chillies, chopped
8 garlic cloves, peeled and halved
1 tablespoon cumin seeds
2 teaspoons fennel seeds
2 teaspoons caraway seeds
3 tablespoons paprika
2 teaspoons ground turmeric
70 g (2½ oz) tomato paste
    (concentrated purée)
2 teaspoons sea salt flakes
800 g (1 lb 12 oz/3¼ cups) tinned tomatoes
2 bay leaves
1 large sea bream, filleted, skin, head, tail
    and bones reserved
handful of coriander (cilantro) leaves,
    chopped

Chraime is usually prepared using whole fish, including the head and tail. In Tel Aviv, grouper is normally the fish of choice, but this is not so readily available in other parts of the world. The good thing about grouper is that it has big bones, so you can remove them from the dish before you put them in your mouth, or at least reduce your risk of choking on a tiny bone. Now, big bones are all well and good, but having to fiddle about removing any bones from your food is still irritating – not to mention fish eyes staring out at you from the sauce. To avoid all this, you can choose to use fish fillets, but chraime actually gets a lot of its flavour from the inclusion of the fish bones. That's why I've come up with the following solution: ask your fishmonger to fillet the whole fish, and to give you the head and bones separately. Then add the bones to a mesh cooking bag, add the bag to the sauce during cooking, and remove before serving for the best of both worlds.

In principle, most saltwater fish have firm enough meat for this dish. I usually buy sea bream, because it yields nice thick fillets and has a flat skeleton that fits easily into a saucepan.

In your pursuit of perfection, don't make the mistake of swapping the tinned tomatoes for fresh varieties. I don't know exactly why, but soups and sauces are always tastier when made with tinned tomatoes. I suspect it's because tomatoes are tinned when fully ripe, whereas those that are exported fresh must be harvested when they're still green and hard. Happily, tinned tomatoes also come pre-skinned and are as cheap as chips.

Roast the capsicums, if desired (see page 298 for instructions).

Heat a generous splash of the oil in a heavy-based frying pan over medium heat. Add the capsicums, chillies and garlic and fry until softened. Meanwhile, grind the whole spices using a mortar and pestle.

Stir the ground cumin, fennel and caraway seeds, and the paprika, turmeric, tomato paste and salt into the vegetable mixture and continue to fry for 1 minute. Add the tinned tomatoes, with their juice, to the pan, then stir in the bay leaves. Break the tomatoes into pieces using a spatula. Seal the fish skin, bones, head and tail in a mesh cooking bag and immerse it in the sauce.

Reduce the heat until the mixture is simmering gently, cover, and continue to cook for 45 minutes.

After 45 minutes, remove the mesh cooking bag from the sauce. If the sauce seems dry, add a dash of water; if it is too loose, mix 1 tablespoon of cornflour (cornstarch) to a paste with some cold water and stir it into the sauce. Add the fish fillets to the sauce and continue to simmer for 15–20 minutes, until just cooked through.

Sprinkle the chraime with chopped coriander and take the pan to the table to serve. Serve with tahini, warm challah bread (page 297) and a cold beer.

1 × quantity tahini (page 282)

2 tablespoons TLV spice mix (page 288)
    or ras el hanout/baharat

600 g (1 lb 5 oz) beef tenderloin (or
    other tender beef cut)

2 tablespoons za'atar

pinch of salt

extra virgin olive oil

1 carrot, thickly sliced

8 small shallots, peeled and halved
    lengthways

4 large garlic cloves, thinly sliced

250 ml (8½ fl oz/1 cup) red wine

2 eggplants (aubergines)

2 each red and yellow capsicums
    (bell peppers)

4 oregano sprigs, leaves picked
    and chopped

1 tablespoon sesame seeds

BEEF TENDERLOIN WITH FIRE-BLACKENED EGGPLANTS AND CAPSICUMS

This is one of my favourite main courses in the book, but it comes with a disclaimer: for days afterwards, you'll be walking around with black soot under your nails. It's almost impossible to get rid of the soot particles that embed themselves under your nails as you peel the blackened vegetables – even a chlorine bath won't do the trick. So, unless you want your guests to see your fingernails and question your hygiene, the only thing for it is to paint your nails.

Almost everything that makes the modern cuisine of Tel Aviv so special comes together in this dish: the intensely smoky flavours of vegetables cooked over fire, the intoxicating aromas of za'atar and Middle Eastern spices, and the finishing touch of velvety tahini.

Slice the beef thinly on the diagonal. Massage the meat with the za'atar, spice mix and salt. Transfer to a bowl, add a generous splash of olive oil, mix well using your hands, then set aside, covered, for at least 1 hour (and ideally 2) to marinate.

Fry the carrot, shallots and garlic in a splash of oil in a heavy-based frying pan for 4–5 minutes. Add the red wine, stir well and bring the mixture to the boil. Reduce the heat until the mixture is simmering, part-cover the pan with a lid, then simmer for 45 minutes, or until the wine has reduced in volume and the sauce has thickened.

Blacken the eggplants and capsicums over the open flame of your hob, or if you do not have a gas stove, under the grill (broiler) (see instructions on pages 298–9). Transfer the blackened capsicums to zip-lock bags and set aside to cool. Leave the blackened eggplants to cool in the open air.

Rinse the capsicums under the cold tap to remove their skin and seeds. Chop into large pieces. Carefully peel the blackened skin from the eggplants (not under the tap!) and cut the flesh into large cubes.

Just before serving, heat a dry frying pan over high heat. Fry the marinated beef, in batches, for 1 minute on each side. Stir in the cooked carrots and shallots, and the eggplant cubes and roasted capsicums.

Divide the tenderloin slices equally among four plates; spoon the vegetables alongside. Drizzle a generous amount of tahini on top. Garnish with the oregano and sesame seeds. (Drink the left-over wine with your meal.)

MATZO BALLS

Makes 12

1.5 litres (51 fl oz/6 cups) chicken soup
  (page 309)
1 × quantity red chrain (page 305)
1 tablespoon schmaltz (page 308)
  or olive oil

2 medium onions, finely chopped
100 g (3½ oz) matzo
3 tablespoons matzo meal
2 eggs
½ bunch flat-leaf (Italian) parsley, leaves
  finely chopped
salt and freshly ground black pepper

From a culinary perspective, the difference between Tel Aviv
and Jerusalem is most obvious during the week of Passover. This
festival commemorates the Israelites' spectacular escape from
Egyptian slavery. According to the Bible, these soon-to-become
Jews were in such a hurry that the bread they baked for the
journey didn't have time to rise. As a result, 1.6 million asylum
seekers *avant la lettre* fled into the desert with matzo in their
knapsacks. In memory of this page in their collective history,
practising Jews refrain from consuming any grain products,
except matzo, for one week. This rabbinic teaching is not strictly
observed everywhere.

In God-fearing Jerusalem, beer taps are shut off and
falafel sellers and pizzeria owners go on forced leave. Kosher
restaurants that are willing to adapt their menu also have to
replace all their contaminated pots, pans, cutlery and crockery.
Tap water is temporarily diverted: spring water is used to flush
metropolitan toilets rather than being drawn from the Sea of
Galilee, just in case fishermen there use bread as bait during
Passover. Really. I'm not making this up.

Over in sinful Tel Aviv, bread baskets are still in full view
on restaurant tables during Passover. Yet Passover is observed
in the city to some extent. In some supermarkets, shelves
with products containing grains are curtained off, and boxes
piled high with matzo are put on display. On the first night of
Passover, the streets are dead, because almost every family is at
home celebrating the Seder together. Stories are told about the
Israelites' exodus from Egypt, the ten plagues, and the parting of
the Red Sea – only then is the matzo soup served, signalling the
start of an extensive meal. By midnight, the cafés are once again
full, the beer is flowing, and people are making up for lost time.

Heat the fat in a frying pan over
medium heat. Add the onions and fry
for 8–10 minutes, until translucent
and softened.

Moisten the matzo under cold running
water for a few seconds – stop before
they become mushy. Crumble the matzo
into a bowl.

Add the matzo meal to the bowl (or blitz
25 g/1 oz of extra matzo to fine crumbs
in a food processor). Add the eggs,
parsley and fried onions and knead
well until the mixture is stiff and well
combined. Season generously with salt
and freshly ground black pepper.

Bring the chicken soup slowly to the boil
in a large saucepan. Meanwhile, using
moist hands, roll the matzo mixture into
balls the size of a ping-pong ball. Lower
them into the boiling soup, in batches if
necessary, turning down the heat until
the soup is just simmering. Cover the
pan and simmer the matzo balls for at
least 15 minutes, so that they take on
the flavours in the soup.

Ladle the chicken soup into bowls,
dividing the matzo balls equally among
the bowls. Serve with the red chrain.

1 tablespoon schmaltz (page 308)
    or olive oil

1–1.5 litres (34–51 fl oz/4–6 cups) chicken
    soup (page 309)
1 large (or 2 small) onions, finely chopped
2 garlic cloves, finely chopped
250 g (9 oz) wholewheat freekeh
splash of aromatic white wine
250 g (9 oz) chestnut mushrooms, cleaned
    and quartered
400 g (14 oz) chicken thigh fillets, diced
150 g (5½ oz/1⅔ cups) chanterelles,
    cleaned and quartered

'RISOTTO' OF FREEKEH WITH CHICKEN AND MUSHROOMS

According to a glorious legend, freekeh was discovered by accident thousands of years ago in the aftermath of an Arab tribal struggle. The winners were thorough: after plundering the losers' possessions, raping their women, and taking their children as slaves, they burned the enemy's grain fields. The entire harvest seemed beyond saving – until one of the survivors found some green grains with a pronounced nutty, smoky flavour among the smouldering remains. The chaff had protected the young, still-moist wheat grains from the scorching fire. Since then, Arab wheat fields have also gone up in smoke in peacetime.

    Although freekeh has been grown and eaten in the holy land for centuries, it's a relatively new phenomenon in Jewish–Israeli cuisine. Celebrity chef Erez Komarovsky learned about freekeh from Israeli Arabs in Galilee and subsequently introduced it to the general public. Nowadays, freekeh is a popular ingredient in trendy restaurants in Tel Aviv, where it is often prepared like a risotto.

Bring the chicken soup to the boil. Turn the heat down until the soup is simmering and cover the pan with a lid.

Heat the fat in a large, heavy-based saucepan over medium heat. Fry the onion until softened and translucent, then stir in the garlic and freekeh until the grains are coated in the fat. Pour in the wine and cook until it has almost all evaporated. Pour in a couple of ladlefuls of the hot soup, stir well, cover again, and simmer gently for 15 minutes, or until the liquid has been absorbed.

Remove the lid from the pan and stir in the mushrooms. Now proceed as with a traditional risotto, adding a ladleful of soup at a time and stirring regularly until the liquid has been absorbed. Keep the heat quite high, as the grains need to steam as they cook.

After 10 minutes, stir in the chicken; after a further 10 minutes, add the chanterelles, continuing to add ladlefuls of the soup as and when necessary during cooking.

The risotto is ready when the freekeh is cooked through but still has a 'bite' to it (more al dente than risotto rice). This should take 40–45 minutes in total. Make sure that the finished risotto is creamy and loose rather than too dry.

Cover the risotto and set aside, off the heat, for 10 minutes before serving – this makes it creamier and more flavourful. Serve warm – but not glowing hot – with the rest of that aromatic white wine.

SCRUMPTIOUS HODGE-PODGE

Think back and tell me honestly: had you even heard of shakshuka seven or eight years ago? Probably not, although as a card-carrying foodie you'll probably find that as difficult to imagine as to admit. Shakshuka has taken the world by storm, and that is mostly down to one man: Yotam Ottolenghi. Through his cookbooks, he has taken every opportunity to place the everyday dish of his homeland on a pedestal.

The world lapped it up eagerly, which in retrospect is no surprise, since shakshuka had international hit written all over it. Firstly, it's a breeze to make, but still looks great. Secondly, despite its exotic appearance, most of its ingredients will already be sitting in the vegetable box of your refrigerator. Thirdly, shakshuka meets two important criteria for modern living: it's both photogenic and (in principle) vegetarian. Furthermore, it fosters good old-fashioned conviviality, because the pan just goes straight on the table and everyone is meant to dig in unabashedly. And lastly there's that fairytale name.

The origins of shakshuka are rooted in Morocco, Tunisia, Algeria and Libya. Originally, vegetables such as artichokes, zucchini (courgettes) and potatoes were cooked down to a thick sauce in the tagine, in which the eggs were later poached. Both in Arabic and in Berber, 'shakshuka' means something like 'hodge-podge'. And that's exactly what it is: a spicy ratatouille with poached eggs.

The North African Jews who fled their land en masse in the 1950s continued to make their beloved shakshuka after their emigration to Israel. They changed the main ingredients, working with the abundance of tomatoes and capsicums (bell peppers) in Israel, but in principle the dish remained the same. For a long time, shakshuka was a dish made in the home, usually for the evening meal. It's only since the nineties that shakshuka has gained popularity in Israeli restaurants not as a dinner, but as a breakfast, lunch, or indeed, brunch, dish.

The undisputed shakshuka temple of Tel Aviv is Dr. Shakshuka. The doctorate degree is not enshrined in Israeli law – or at least not when it concerns shakshuka. In any case, no one begrudges owner Bino Gabso for co-opting the name of his restaurant for himself.

In 1991 Gabso, the son of Libyan immigrants, took over his father's restaurant in the centre of Jaffa. He decided to specialise in the family recipe that he had perfected in prison in Israel. The story has been told so many times that it now has a place in Israeli folklore, but the large, heavily perspiring gentleman that you'll immediately recognise from the restaurant's logo will gladly recount the whole tale again in technicolour. Most days, you'll find him at the back of his restaurant, sitting at a table for two (which, given his size, instantly becomes a table for one). The details of the story may vary according to the day on which you catch him, but this is the version he told to me.

In addition to his restaurant Gabso's father had an illegal money-exchange office, where the young Bino did favours for him. After every successful deal, his father rewarded him with a pan of homemade shakshuka. One day, Bino was caught red-handed. To everyone's surprise, instead of fining him for this misdemeanour, the judge decided to make an example of him and sentenced him to fifteen months in prison. In prison, Bino soon started making shakshuka for the prisoners and guards. It was such a hit that the prison warden supplied him with a gas burner and daily fresh ingredients. His fellow inmates started to call him Dr. Shakshuka – and the rest is history.

Dr. Shakshuka became the most famous restaurant in Jaffa. Over the quarter-century that it's been in business, this small establishment on the edge of the flea market has expanded several times in a haphazard way: every time an adjoining restaurant was put up for sale, Gabso bought it and incorporated it into his existing restaurant. Which explains why Dr. Shakshuka is a patchwork of different rooms, all decorated with a hodge-podge of second-hand items from the flea market – the perfect setting in which to enjoy a scrumptious shakshuka.

Serves 2–4

2 teaspoons TLV spice mix (page 288)
   or ras el hanout/baharat

500 g (1 lb 2 oz/2½ cups) diced vine tomatoes
olive oil for frying
2 small onions, finely chopped
2 Romano capsicums (peppers), stalks
   removed, deseeded, flesh diced
2 garlic cloves, crushed
2 teaspoons harissa
2 teaspoons za'atar
1 bay leaf
pinch of salt
4–8 eggs, separated
2 mint sprigs, leaves roughly chopped
pinch of sumac
warm, soft bread, such as challah
   (page 297) to serve

Drain the diced tomatoes in a colander while you prepare the vegetables.

Heat a splash of olive oil in a wide, heavy-based frying pan over medium heat. Add the onions, peppers, garlic and harissa, stir well and fry for 1–2 minutes. Add the tomatoes, za'atar, spice mix and bay leaf and stir again. Bring the mixture to a gentle simmer and continue to cook for 15–20 minutes, until the tomatoes have broken down and the sauce has thickened. Season with salt.

If you want to serve individual portions of shakshuka, then at this stage, divide the sauce among several smaller pans. Otherwise, leave it where it is. Remove the bay leaf from the sauce, then add the egg whites to the sauce, stirring a little to break them up if they have all congregated in one place. When the egg whites are cooked through, carefully top them with the egg yolks and sprinkle each with a pinch of salt. Cook for 1 minute longer, then turn off the heat and set aside for 2 minutes. Just before serving, garnish with the mint leaves. Serve the shakshuka in the pan with warm bread alongside.

See photo on page 186.

SHAKSHUKA WITH TOMATO AND SWEET CAPSICUMS

Frankly, restaurant versions of shakshuka can often be disappointing. Even in eateries like Dr. Shakshuka or Shakshukia, where shakshuka is the speciality, it's never quite as good as at home. That's first and foremost because finely dicing restaurant quantities of fresh tomatoes is a time-consuming (not to mention costly) affair – most kitchens prefer to use tinned tomatoes or passata (puréed tomatoes) for convenience and value. Although I'm generally a big fan of tinned tomatoes and other conserves, when it comes to shakshuka I think it's important to use fresh ingredients.

A second, more difficult problem with restaurant shakshuka concerns the eggs, which are, more often than not, served overdone. In order to fully enjoy your shakshuka, a runny yolk is essential: part of the pleasure of the dish is breaking the egg yolk and watching the yellow liquid meander over the sauce, then scooping it into soft bread before it sets. Restaurant chefs know this, but because time is against them, the lid usually goes on the pan. At best, this results in eggs topped with unsightly pale membranes; at worst, it produces criminally overcooked egg yolks. Even if your eggs are cooked to perfection in the pan, said pan will then be placed under a warming lamp, where they will continue to cook until the orders of your table companions are ready.

I have a simple trick for getting perfectly cooked eggs every time: just separate the eggs and cook the whites first, adding the yolks at the last minute. Serve as soon as they are heated through.

SHAKSHUKA WITH ENGLISH SPINACH AND FETA

Serves 2–6

Shakshuka is not a strict dish; as long as eggs are cooked in a pan with braised vegetables, anything goes – although in M25 I ate a shakshuka in which even the eggs had been replaced, with calf brains. A popular alternative to the well-known red shakshukah is the green version, made with English spinach instead of tomatoes. This version is the one to order if you're in almost any restaurant with more than one shakshuka on the menu.

knob of butter
olive oil
2 garlic cloves, finely chopped
1 green chilli, deseeded and thinly sliced
   into rings
1 large leek, trimmed, sliced into rings
400 g (14 oz/8 cups) spinach
salt and freshly ground black pepper
4–8 eggs, separated
100 g (3½ oz/⅔ cup) feta, crumbled
warm soft bread, such as challah
   (page 297) to serve

Heat the butter and a dash of olive oil in a large frying pan over medium heat. Add the garlic, chilli and leek and fry for 1–2 minutes, stirring frequently.

Stir in the spinach and a good pinch of salt and cook for 2–3 minutes, or until wilted.

If you want to serve individual portions of shakshuka, then at this stage, divide the sauce among several smaller pans. Otherwise, leave it where it is. Add the egg whites to the sauce, stirring a little to break them up if they have all congregated in one place. When the egg whites are cooked through, carefully top them with the egg yolks, crumble over the feta and season with salt (remember that the feta will already be salty). Cook for 1 minute longer, then turn off the heat and set aside for 2 minutes. Just before serving, season with plenty of freshly ground black pepper. Serve the shakshuka in the pan with warm bread alongside.

Serves 2–3

5 roasted garlic cloves (page 286)
1 × quantity tahini with roasted
    garlic (page 282)

5 medium vine tomatoes, diced
1 large eggplant (aubergine)
2 red or yellow capsicums
    (bell peppers)
olive oil
1 large onion, finely chopped
1 teaspoon harissa
2 teaspoons za'atar
1 teaspoon smoked paprika
1 smoked chicken fillet, diced
pinch of salt
4–6 eggs, separated
pinch of sumac
warm, soft bread, such as challah
    (page 297) to serve

SMOKY SHAKSHUKA WITH CHICKEN AND EGGPLANT

The North African immigrants who introduced shakshuka in Israel would cook it in the evening as a reward for a day's hard work. It was only much later, after Israeli restaurants adopted the dish, that it started being associated with breakfast and brunch. Once traditional shakshuka had become established as a breakfast dish, restaurants that specialised in shakshuka had to come up with more filling variations to attract evening trade, and they usually did this by adding the likes of minced (ground) meat, merguez, shawarma or smoked chicken breast. At Machneyuda, a restaurant in Jerusalem with a Tel Avivian spirit, celebrity chef Assaf Granit devised *hamshuka*, an inspired shakshuka made with minced meat, hummus, labneh, pickled lemons and tahini. Most decent shakshuka restaurants now have a version of hamshuka on their menu.

I fill my evening shakshuka with as many smoky flavours as possible: flame-roasted vegetables, smoked chicken, sticky roasted garlic and smoked paprika. I often make it before I go out for the night and I always make too much on purpose – the leftovers are perfect for soothing a hefty hangover the next morning.

Drain the diced tomatoes in a colander. Meanwhile, blacken the eggplant and capsicums over the open flame of your hob, or if you do not have a gas stove, in the oven under the grill (broiler) (see instructions on pages 298–299). Seal the blackened capsicums in zip-lock bags and set aside to cool. Set the eggplant aside to cool in the open air.

Heat a dash of olive oil in a frying pan over medium heat and fry the onion with the harissa, za'atar and smoked paprika for 3–4 minutes, stirring well. When the onions have softened and are translucent, stir in the tomatoes and cover the pan. Reduce the heat to low and continue to cook for 15 minutes, or until the tomatoes have broken down to a thick sauce.

Meanwhile, remove the stalk and blackened skin from the eggplant and the skin, stalk and seeds from the capsicums. Slice the capsicums into strips and the eggplant into cubes.

Remove the lid from the pan and add the roasted garlic, smoked chicken, eggplant and capsicums to the simmering sauce. Season with a good pinch of salt.

If you want to serve individual portions of shakshuka, then at this stage, divide the sauce among several smaller pans. Otherwise, leave it where it is. Add the egg whites to the sauce, stirring a little to break them up if they have all congregated in one place. When the egg whites are cooked through, carefully top them with the egg yolks and season with salt. Cook for 1 minute longer, then turn off the heat and set aside for 2 minutes. Just before serving, sprinkle the shakshuka with sumac and drizzle with the tahini. Serve the shakshuka in the pan with warm bread alongside.

KOSHER BEEF 'TAGLIATA'

Serves 4

1 tablespoon za'atar

500 g (1 lb 2 oz) shoulder tender
  (beef shoulder petite tender; see
  introduction)

90 ml (3 fl oz) extra virgin olive oil

2 tablespoons red wine vinegar

1 teaspoon chilli flakes

1 teaspoon sea salt flakes (optional)

250 g (9 oz/1¼ cups) cherry tomatoes,
  halved

10 oregano sprigs

In Dutch, the 'shoulder tender' (beef shoulder petite tender) cut of beef (from the chuck shoulder clod) is called *jodenhaas*, which means 'Jewish fillet'. The origin of this word can be traced back to a highly surreal Bible story. After years of living in exile, Jacob, the father of the Israelites, returns to his childhood home with his four wives and twelve children. On the way he meets a mysterious man-cum-angel with whom he wrestles for a night. Although Jacob twists his hip during the struggle, he wins – and refuses to let the man go until he blesses Jacob. The man blesses him with a new name: Israel. The dietary upshot of this rather bizarre story is that to this day, out of respect for Jacob's/Israel's injuries, Jews are not allowed to eat meat that comes from the cow's hindquarters.

Because removing all forbidden bits of meat is a labour-intensive job, all kosher butchers choose to sell the entire hindquarter to their non-kosher colleagues out of convenience. The non-kosher butchers think that this is a great deal, because the most tender cuts – beef tenderloin, rump steak, entrecôte, filet mignon and sirloin steak – are found in the haunch. These are the cuts that orthodox Jews must forgo, contenting themselves with the tougher stewing cuts from the forelegs. There is, however, one prized cut from the forequarters of the cow: the shoulder tender (*jodenhaas*). This kosher steak is a forgotten cut that is becoming increasingly appreciated by gourmets, because it's just as tender as, but much more flavourful than tenderloin.

The quality of this cut depends on its size, as well as on the breed of cattle, its age, what the animal has been fed, and the terroir. Quiz your butcher on these points before you buy, or ask his advice. Only the best-quality shoulder tender is worth eating raw – and then it's among the most delicious meat you can eat.

Rub the za'atar into the meat and set aside.

Whisk the olive oil, vinegar, chilli flakes and salt, if using, together in a large bowl until emulsified. (Do not add salt to kosher meat, which will already have been salted by the butcher.)

Cut the meat into thin slices. Flatten each a little by bashing it with the palm of your hand.

Add the beef slices, tomatoes and the leaves from 8 sprigs of oregano to the bowl of vinaigrette. Cover and marinate in the refrigerator for at least 2 hours.

At least an hour before serving, remove the bowl from the refrigerator to allow the meat time to come up to room temperature. Taste and season with more salt if necessary.

To serve, arrange the beef slices onto a platter and spoon over the tomatoes and the rest of the vinaigrette marinade from the bowl. Garnish with the reserved oregano leaves. Serve with a fruity red or rosé wine.

Makes enough to feed an army

MEATBALLS (ENOUGH FOR 1.5 L/ 51 FL OZ/6 CUPS SOUP)

300 g (10½ oz) minced (ground) beef

1 egg

1 teaspoon paprika

1 teaspoon allspice

1 teaspoon harissa

2 tablespoons dry breadcrumbs
  or Japanese panko

SOUP

4 litres (135 fl oz/16 cups) left-over
  beef-tongue stock (page 141)

1.2 kg (2 lb 10 oz/5 cups) tinned peeled
  tomatoes

210 g (7½ oz) tomato paste
  (concentrated purée)

2–3 beef stock (bouillon) cubes

a few pinches of salt

a few pinches of sugar

30 g (1 oz/¼ cup) cornflour (cornstarch)

SMOKY TOMATO SOUP WITH MEATBALLS

In my recipe for smoked beef tongue with beetroot and quail eggs, I simmer the tongue in a powerfully flavoured broth. The great thing about that dish is that the same broth can then be used to make this quick but hearty soup with a unique smoky flavour.

The best way to make this dish is when you have left-over meatballs in the freezer, just waiting to be added to the stock. This trick not only makes your life easier, but also results in firmer meatballs – frozen meatballs hold together better in the broth than freshly made ones.

This recipe makes enough soup to eat every day for a week with your extended family or selected neighbours. Freeze the rest in portions – it will keep in the freezer for several months.

In a bowl, mix together all of the meatballs ingredients. Using moist hands, roll equal-sized meatballs from the mixture, then transfer them to a baking tray, cover with plastic wrap and freeze until needed.

Bring the left-over beef-tongue stock to the boil in a very large saucepan and add the tinned tomatoes in their juice, and the tomato paste. Remove the pan from the heat and set aside to cool slightly, then purée the mixture using a hand-held blender. Season the soup with the stock cubes, salt and sugar.

Mix the cornflour to a smooth paste with a little water. Gradually blend it into the soup using the hand-held blender.

Return the pan of soup to the heat and bring to a simmer. Slide the frozen meatballs into the boiling soup 15 minutes before serving and simmer in the soup until piping hot and cooked through.

ROMANO'S
FISH SHAWARMA

As if he doesn't already have enough on his plate, chef Eyal Shani keeps opening new restaurants. When I visited Tel Aviv for this book, Shani's latest venture was called Romano, and finding it was half the battle. We were dropped off by our taxi driver on the busy thoroughfare between downtown Tel Aviv and the old fishing port of Jaffa, a filthy road whose shabby shop fronts display clothes that were in fashion about a decade ago. At first glance we couldn't make out a single restaurant, but after walking up and down the road a few times, we discovered an inconspicuous-looking side passage leading to a courtyard overlooked by a dilapidated apartment complex. It was packed with people sitting at long tables laden with pizza and beer, with a DJ to keep things lively.

We asked for Romano and were directed to a barely lit staircase. At the top, a tattooed boy with artistic facial hair and flesh tunnels for earlobes guided us through the packed dining room to a table on the balcony with views of the courtyard, where we were the only guests. It was almost 9pm, but in Tel Aviv dinner starts later than even in Barcelona or Buenos Aires. When we left, it was after midnight, but the entrance staircase was full of young guests waiting, glass in hand, for a table.

Romano had the distinct feel of a pop-up. Pretty soon, developers will probably have taken charge of the building and Romano will be gone. That would be a travesty, because the first dish I ate there, sea bass shawarma, was so good that I want to eat it every time I visit Tel Aviv. On my next visit, I lamented on that balcony, I'll no doubt find a chic redevelopment where Romano once stood, full of the rich diaspora Jews who are steadily pricing ordinary Tel Avivians out of the city. Our hip waiter heard me sighing and reassured me that Romano is here to stay. I wanted to believe him, but just to be on the safe side, I invited myself into the restaurant's kitchen so that I could crib the recipe for that fish shawarma.

4 sea bass fillets, skin on
sea salt flakes
extra virgin olive oil
2 large, firm beef tomatoes, roughly
    chopped
1 green chilli
1 red onion, cut in half and thinly sliced
    into half moons
½ bunch of flat-leaf (Italian) parsley,
    roughly chopped
½ bunch of dill, roughly chopped
handful of rocket (arugula) (same amount
    as the herbs), roughly chopped
120 g (4½ oz/½ cup) full-fat yoghurt
salt and freshly ground black pepper

Make sure all the ingredients are at room temperature before you start.

Score the skin of the fish fillets several times using a sharp knife.
Season with salt and drizzle with olive oil. Set aside.

Purée the tomatoes with a pinch of salt using a hand-held blender.
Thanks to the pectin in the tomatoes, it will quickly thicken to a sauce.

Remove the stalk from the chilli, then roll it back and forth between your
palms, shaking out the seeds as you go. Slice the chilli into thin rings.

Heat a chargrill pan or non-stick frying pan over the highest heat
possible until smoking hot – for this dish to be a success, the skin of
the fish fillets must be super crisp. Chargrill the fish fillets, skin-side
down, for 3–4 minutes – when the edges of the fish fillets turn white,
turn them over carefully and continue to chargrill for 1–2 minutes,
until just cooked through. (If the fish skin sticks to the pan when you
turn over the fish fillets, carefully pull it loose and set aside with the
chopped vegetables.)

Cut the fillets (and crisp skin) into thin strips using a sharp knife. Toss
the fish carefully with the chilli, onion, herbs and rocket.

To serve, spoon some of the tomato sauce into the centre of four plates
and smear it artistically. Dot with the yoghurt. Divide the fish mixture
equally among the plates. Drizzle with olive oil and season with salt and
freshly ground black pepper. Serve immediately.

ZA'ATAR OMELETTE WITH GOAT'S CHEESE AND HONEYED WALNUTS

Twenty-five years ago, when the prospect of peace in the Middle East was easier to imagine than a decent dinner in Tel Aviv, people around the world were familiar with the Israeli-style breakfast, a meal that originated in the kibbutzes, the socialist agricultural settlements whose residents shared everything. The residents would get up before daybreak to work the land, after which they would sit down together to a breakfast made with the produce they had just harvested. In the 1950s and 1960s, luxury hotels copied this healthy start to the day. Following the declaration of the Jewish state, Israel's tourism industry grew exponentially, mainly due to the massive influx of tourists from the Jewish diaspora. Because many of these Jewish tourists attached huge importance to the rites and symbols of their religion, new resorts were built whose restaurants were, without exception, kosher. As a result, cold meats suddenly became taboo at breakfast: Jewish dietary laws forbid the combination of meat and dairy products. To compensate for this loss, an abundance of fresh fruit, salads, soft cheeses and egg dishes were introduced to the breakfast spread.

Nowadays Tel Aviv is in a league of its own when it comes to lunch and dinner, but there is still no substitute for the Israeli-style breakfast. In every back street you'll find a café or restaurant serving Israeli breakfasts from the crack of dawn. However, you don't have to be an early riser to enjoy an Israeli breakfast – you can order it in the middle of the night if you wish, from branches of the 24/7 Benedict chain, for example.

A standard Israeli breakfast (*aruhat bokker*) consists of coffee, freshly squeezed orange juice, warm bread, Israeli salad, a selection of soft cheeses, tuna salad, tahini, a bowl of olives and a rich herb omelette similar to an Italian frittata, although frittata is never eaten for breakfast. People say that breakfast is the most important meal of the day, and Israelis certainly don't take this lightly.

Serves 1

½ × quantity quick Israeli salad (page 291)

3 eggs
1 tablespoon milk
1 tablespoon chopped chives
1 teaspoon za'atar
salt and freshly ground black pepper
15 g (½ oz) butter
25 g (1 oz/¼ cup) walnuts, coarsely
    chopped
1 teaspoon honey
50 g (1¾ oz/⅓ cup) semi-soft goat's cheese
    or feta, crumbled
pinch of sumac

Briefly beat the eggs with the milk, chives and za'atar, then season with salt and pepper.

Set a frying pan over medium heat. Add the butter and swirl it around the pan as it melts. Pour in the egg mixture, swirl the pan to evenly distribute it, then cook for 20 seconds. Reduce the heat to its lowest setting, then continue to cook the omelette slowly.

Meanwhile, toast the walnuts in a separate, dry frying pan over high heat. Keep an eye on the walnuts as they will burn easily. Remove the pan from the heat as soon as the walnuts begin to colour, then drizzle with the honey. Return the pan to the heat and continue to cook the honeyed nuts until lightly caramelised.

When the omelette is nearly cooked through, pile the goat's cheese and honeyed nuts onto one side of it, then fold the rest of the omelette over the filling. Slide the omelette onto a plate, garnish with the sumac and serve with the Israeli salad.

DARK-CHOCOLATE HALVA

100 g (3½ oz/⅔ cup) dark chocolate
   (minimum 70% cocoa solids), chopped
400 g (14 oz/1½ cups) raw tahini
120 ml (4 fl oz/½ cup) cold water
350 g (12½ oz/1⅔ cups) sugar
1 vanilla pod, split lengthways, seeds
   scraped out and reserved

Halva is made from raw tahini and sugar. It's a bit like marzipan, but with a more grainy texture and a richer flavour. Israeli restaurants will often treat you to a cube of halva – usually factory-produced stuff – when they bring the bill. This synthetic halva has given the sweet treat a bad name among foodies who have never tasted the real thing. For a long time, I was one of them.

The strange thing about thinking you don't like something is that you can go without testing the hypothesis for years, even decades. Why would you put something in your mouth that you believe to be gross? It's often your peers who pressure you into trying the food again. In my case this was at the market in Tel Aviv. There were dozens of flavours of halva, some as big as cheeses, laid out on display. They looked pretty delicious and a world away from the shrink-wrapped stuff of my teenage years that had saddled me with a lifelong dislike of halva. At the front of his stall, the vendor had set out free samples of halva and was busy loudly promoting the virtues of each. My Dutch companion, on holiday in Israel for the first time, fell upon them without hesitation, so I followed suit. Man, they were nice.

Making halva yourself is not difficult, provided you have a digital sugar thermometer. The first time is the most fiddly, but once you get used to making it, you can put all that energy into thinking up original flavours. Try, for example, mixing poppy seeds through the halva mixture instead of chocolate. Or toasted pecans. Or crumbled gingerbread. The possibilities are endless.

Line a high-sided 20 cm (8 in) square or 25 cm × 16 cm (9¾ in × 6¼ in) dish with baking paper. If the dish you have is any smaller, make sure it has very high sides (or use two).

Melt the chocolate in a bain-marie. Keep warm so that the chocolate stays liquid while you make the sugar syrup. Scoop the tahini into a large mixing bowl and set aside.

Bring the water, sugar and vanilla seeds to the boil in a heavy-based saucepan, stirring until the sugar has completely dissolved. Then remove the spoon from the pan and do not stir it again. Continue to boil the sugar syrup for about 10 minutes, until the temperature on a sugar thermometer reads exactly 245°F (118°C) – take the reading in Fahrenheit if possible, as this is more accurate than Celsius. Do not leave the sugar syrup unattended and be very careful: molten sugar can cause serious burns.

As soon as the sugar syrup has come up to temperature, remove the pan carefully from the heat. Work quickly: using an electric mixer set to medium speed, gradually pour the sugar syrup onto the tahini in the mixing bowl in a thin stream, beating continuously and taking care not to splash yourself. Do not mix longer than necessary. When all of the sugar syrup has been incorporated and the mixture is smooth, fold in the melted chocolate to create a marbled effect.

Transfer the halva mixture to the lined dish and spread with a spatula into an even layer. Cover the halva with another sheet of baking paper and press down with your hands. Remove the top sheet of baking paper and set the halva aside to cool. Be patient as it is best eaten at room temperature. The halva will keep for at least a week in an airtight container at room temperature.

EYAL'S FAMOUS BABY CAULIFLOWER

It is hard to believe that before 1950 – the year carpaccio was invented, in Venice – no cook had ever thought to serve thinly sliced raw meat. Or that before the Earl of Sandwich, no one had been smart enough to fit a meal between two slices of bread. And, in the same vein, did five millennia of culinary civilisation really pass us by before an Israeli chef came up with the bright idea of grilling a cauliflower in its entirety? In fact, the global rehabilitation of the cauliflower's image began in Tel Aviv. It was chef Eyal Shani who, back in 2008, put his baby cauliflower ('melting into itself') on the menu at his HaSalon and North Abraxass restaurants. It quickly became his signature dish, and had to feature on the menus of each new restaurant he subsequently opened. Jamie Oliver spotted the dish and popularised it; variations on it have since been served in restaurants all over the world.

According to *The New York Times*, which devoted a longform article to Shani's original grilled cauliflower, the hype around this dish is down to the fact that it's a similar experience to eating a piece of meat: the burnished, golden-brown exterior of the cauliflower gives way to a silky, tender core. What's more, grilled cauliflower has the edge on other grilled vegetables because it pairs perfectly with wine, especially Meursault, Grüner Veltliner or a not-too-young Riesling.

Serves 2–4

1 × quantity tahini (page 282)

2 small cauliflowers, leaves intact
    (about 600 g/1 lb 5 oz in total)
extra virgin olive oil
sea salt flakes

Preheat the oven to 250°C (480°F) and switch the grill (broiler) to its highest setting.

Bring a large saucepan of salted water to the boil (approximately 2 teaspoons of salt per litre of water). Place the cauliflowers, leaves still intact, upside down in the pan. Boil for 5 minutes (start the timer as soon as the cauliflowers are submerged).

Drain the cauliflowers. Grease your hands with olive oil then massage the oil into the cauliflowers. Sprinkle all over with the salt. Crumple two sheets of baking paper into balls, then spread each one out a little, to create nests in which to sit the cauliflowers. Roast the cauliflowers under the grill for 20–25 minutes, until the outermost parts start to blacken.

Remove the cauliflowers from the oven and drizzle generously all over with a thin stream of olive oil (this should be absorbed by the cauliflowers). Season again with more salt flakes if desired. Serve the cauliflowers in their baking-paper nests, with a bowl of tahini alongside for dipping (and a glass of white wine).

Serves 4

2 fennel bulbs
extra virgin olive oil
2 tablespoons maple syrup
sea salt flakes to season
1 orange, thickly sliced
splash of arak or ouzo
1 teaspoon fennel seeds
150 g (5½ oz/1 cup) blanched almonds
2 tablespoons almond oil
2 tablespoons lemon juice
4 pinches of sumac

CARAMELISED FENNEL AND ORANGE WITH ARAK AND ALMOND TAHINI

On the periphery of the impressive tahini section of a sustainable supermarket in Tel Aviv, I encountered a special tahini made not from sesame seeds but from almonds. Intrigued, I bought a large jar and took it home in my suitcase. Ten miles high, the worries started to niggle at me. What if I fell in love with the almond tahini? Then I would run out of it in a matter of days and wouldn't have access to it again until my next trip to Tel Aviv, which was over a month away. Could I make it myself, I wondered? After all, you don't need a millstone to grind almonds, just a food processor. Almonds are slightly less oily than sesame seeds, but that problem could be solved with the addition of a few extra drops of oil. At home, I got to work immediately, and instantly fell in love with the result. And that jar of almond tahini from Tel Aviv? It's still in my pantry, unopened.

Preheat the oven to 250°C (480°F) (turn off the fan if you have one) and switch the grill (broiler) to its highest setting. Line a baking tray with baking paper.

Bring 1 litre (34 fl oz/4 cups) of water and 2 teaspoons of salt to the boil in a large saucepan. Halve the fennel bulbs lengthways and remove the root. Suspend a steaming basket over the pan of boiling water and place the fennel halves, cut-sides down, inside. Cover the pan and steam the fennel for 10–12 minutes, until al dente.

Remove the lid from the pan to release the steam and allow the fennel to cool. After a couple of minutes, rub the fennel halves all over with the oil and maple syrup, and sprinkle with the salt.

Arrange the orange slices onto the prepared baking tray, drizzle with the arak and sprinkle with the fennel seeds and a little salt. Add the fennel halves and grill for 15–20 minutes, until the fennel and orange slices are deep golden brown. Remove from the oven and set aside to cool.

Reduce the oven temperature to 180°C (350°F). Put the almonds onto a roasting tray and toast for 4–5 minutes, shaking the tray occasionally during cooking, until they are a pale golden colour (don't let them turn golden brown). Transfer the almonds to a food processor and grind as finely as possible. With the motor still running, gradually add the almond oil, then the lemon juice; continue to blend for at least 5 minutes until the mixture comes together as a paste that resembles raw tahini. With the motor still running, add drops of cold water to the mixture as necessary, until the almond tahini has a thick, creamy consistency. Season with salt.

To serve, spread a generous amount of almond tahini onto four plates. Top with the roasted fennel and orange, and drizzle with olive oil. Garnish with the sumac.

Serves 4

juice of 5 limes
85 ml (2¾ fl oz/⅓ cup) arak or ouzo
1 cm (½ in) piece of ginger,
    peeled and halved
1 garlic clove, chopped
pinch of salt
1 pink grapefruit, peeled and segmented
1 ripe avocado, peeled, pitted and sliced
400 g (14 oz) skinless sushi-grade
    salmon fillet, thinly sliced
1 red chilli, deseeded and thinly sliced
    into rings
4 mint sprigs, leaves chopped
2 tablespoons pine nuts, toasted

SALMON CEVICHE WITH AVOCADO, GRAPEFRUIT AND ARAK

Ceviche is incredibly popular in Tel Aviv. During long, humid summer evenings in the city, the semi-raw fish dish is just the sort of light, fresh meal that people crave. What's more, its simplicity – spanking fresh fish cooked briefly in citrus juice – is completely in tune with the style of modern Israeli chefs. By using typical Middle Eastern ingredients, these chefs make the Latin American dish their own. These two fusion ceviches that I thought up are a cross between Tel Aviv and Lima.

Mix the lime juice, arak, ginger, garlic and salt in a non-metallic bowl. Stir well and set aside for 2 minutes to allow the flavours to mingle. Strain the marinade through a fine-mesh sieve into a clean bowl.

Cut each of the grapefruit segments in half lengthways to create two thinner segments. Sprinkle the avocado slices with a little salt and drizzle with 1 teaspoon of the marinade. Cut the salmon with a very sharp knife into very thin slices. Marinate the salmon slices in the marinade for 2 minutes.

Divide the marinated salmon slices equally among four plates and drizzle with a little of the marinade. Garnish with the avocado, grapefruit, chilli, mint and pine nuts (you will probably have more avocado and chilli than you need).

SEA BASS CEVICHE WITH ROASTED EGGPLANT

Roast the eggplants over the open flame of your hob, or if you do not have a gas stove, under the grill (broiler) (see instructions on page 299). Set the eggplants aside to cool slightly, then carefully peel away the blackened skin. Cut both eggplants in half lengthways and put one eggplant half onto each plate, cut-side facing upwards. Cover each plate with plastic wrap and press down on the eggplant with the palms of your hands to flatten it against the plate. Remove the plastic wrap and drizzle each eggplant half with olive oil. Season with salt.

Mix the lime juice, ginger, garlic, a pinch of salt and the contents of the teabag in a non-metallic bowl. Set aside for 2 minutes, then remove the pieces of ginger and garlic. Set the marinade aside for a further 5 minutes, then strain it through a fine-mesh sieve into a clean bowl.

Cut the sea bass fillets into very thin slices using a sharp knife. Sprinkle with salt, then marinate for 2 minutes.

Arrange the marinated sea bass slices on top of the eggplant. Drizzle with some of the marinade. Garnish with the chilli, smoked almonds and coriander leaves.

Serves 4

2 eggplants (aubergines)
extra virgin olive oil
sea salt flakes
juice of 6 limes
1 cm (½ in) piece of ginger, peeled
    and halved
1 garlic clove, halved
1½ teaspoons lapsang souchong tea leaves
    (about the contents of 1 teabag)
500 g (1 lb 2 oz) skinless sea bass fillets,
    pin bones removed
1 red chilli, deseeded and thinly sliced
    into rings
30 g (1 oz/¼ cup) smoked salted almonds,
    sliced into slivers
4 coriander (cilantro) sprigs, leaves only

CHALLAH PUDDING WITH ADVOCAAT-MASCARPONE SAUCE

According to the United Nations, global food waste must be halved by 2030. A considerable chunk of this excess food can be blamed on the Jews, namely the Yiddish *momme*, who defines herself through the cooking of excessive amounts of food. When my dyed-in-the-wool Dutch mother-in-law pushes the boat out and everything gets eaten up, it's something to celebrate. For my own mum, empty dishes signal code red: there wasn't enough! To prevent this, she always makes ridiculous quantities of food, and inevitably copious amounts of leftovers remain. These are always packed away in the refrigerator in plastic containers with the best of intentions, only to grow multi-coloured fungus in the weeks that follow.

I have inherited the tendency to cook too much food from my mum. Certainly on Saturdays at Shabbat brunch – a meal that involves a lot of bread and a lot of guests (some expected, some not) – I prefer to make too much rather than risk it being too little. Just the idea of running out of bread halfway through the meal gives me chills. So I will either bake or buy two extra loaves of challah, and prepare double the required amount of salads. Those salads do get eaten up over the course of the weekend, but the surplus bread mountain is insurmountable.

The most logical way of using up left-over bread is to let it dry and blitz it into breadcrumbs. But because the human need for breadcrumbs is also finite, I have come up with this challah pudding with an addictively delicious sauce. Problem solved; UN officials happy. Or so I thought. Only that my challah pudding is so popular with my children that they now look forward to it all week. So now, on Fridays, I make an extra challah loaf. Just to be sure I have enough left over.

Serves 12

PUDDING
65 g (2¼ oz/½ cup) raisins
100–110 ml (3½–4 fl oz) rum
4 eggs
100 ml (3½ fl oz) full-cream (whole) milk
125 ml (4 fl oz/½ cup) thick cream (double/heavy)
60 g (2 oz/¼ cup) caster (superfine) sugar
1 teaspoon ground cinnamon
pinch of salt
400 g (14 oz) stale challah (or other soft, enriched bread such as brioche), torn into small pieces
85 g (3 oz/⅔ cup) walnuts, halved
knob of butter, at room temperature

SAUCE
100 g (3½ oz/½ cup) mascarpone
60 ml (2 fl oz/¼ cup) advocaat
2 teaspoons lime juice
50 ml (1¾ fl oz) thick cream (double/heavy)

Soak the raisins in the rum in a non-metallic bowl for at least 1 hour. Meanwhile, grease and line a 30 cm (12 in) cake tin. Beat the eggs, milk, cream, sugar, cinnamon and salt in a large bowl. Add the challah pieces to the mixture and set aside to soak for 30 minutes.

Preheat the oven to 170°C (340°F). Drain the raisins (reserving the rum) and fold them into the bread mixture along with the walnuts. Pour the bread mixture into the prepared cake tin and smooth the top to even it out. Drizzle over the reserved rum and bake in the oven for 1 hour.

Meanwhile, for the sauce, blend the mascarpone, advocaat and lime juice until smooth using a hand-held blender. Add the whipped cream and pulse briefly to combine. (The sauce will keep in the refrigerator for 3–4 days.)

Remove the challah pudding from the oven and set aside to cool in the tin for a few minutes before serving (or leave to cool completely). Serve lukewarm or cold in slices, with the sauce. Be aware that the hotter the pudding, the more quickly the sauce will melt and slide onto your plate.

MALABI

At the epicentre of culinary Tel Aviv, where four streets (Carmel Market, Allenby Street, King George Street and bar-heavy Sheinkin) meet, it's still very busy after midnight. The view, overlooking an old petrol station and the rubbish from the day's market, may not be very inspiring, but nevertheless this is where the city's night owls come together for a tipsy conversation, a game of *shesh besh* (backgammon) and the local speciality, malabi. Tonight, I have eaten out in the neighbourhood, but I consciously skipped dessert in order to indulge here.

In Israel, this creamy milk pudding is called malabi, but the original Arabic name is *muhallebi* and, to bring the confusion full circle, the little kiosk I'm standing in front of has the name Hamalabia. You'll find this sort of malabi hole-in-the-wall everywhere in Tel Aviv, especially in the narrow streets of Jaffa, and the concept is more or less universal: glasses of malabi stand in the refrigerator, ready to be covered with your choice of flavoured syrup, plus a topping such as chopped hazelnuts, pistachios or grated coconut. Although I don't have a sweet tooth and am certainly not a pudding fanatic, I have completely fallen for this simple dessert – especially at this location, where your malabi comes with a free cup of Turkish coffee (and the feeling that the night is still young).

Serves 8

1 litre (34 fl oz/4 cups) full-cream (whole) milk
100 g (3½ oz) sugar
250 ml (8½ fl oz/1 cup) thick cream (double/ heavy)
2 tablespoons rosewater
75 g (2½ oz) cornflour (cornstarch)
50 g (1¾ oz/⅓ cup) pistachios
100 ml (3½ fl oz) pomegranate cordial (grenadine)
drizzle of pomegranate molasses (optional)
3 tablespoons grated coconut

Bring about three-quarters of the milk and all of the sugar and cream to the boil in a large, heavy-based saucepan.

Meanwhile, whisk the remaining milk to a smooth paste with the rosewater and the cornflour. Pour this mixture into the hot milk mixture and reduce the heat slightly. Stir continuously until the mixture thickens – this will happen just as you start to think it will never become thicker. Continue stirring for just over 1 minute, then remove the pan from the heat and pour the mixture into 8 heatproof glasses, covering each immediately with plastic wrap (this will prevent a skin from forming).

Set aside to cool, then chill in the refrigerator for at least 2–3 hours, or preferably half a day.

Toast the pistachios in a dry frying pan until they start to colour. Transfer to a bowl and set aside to cool, then chop them roughly.

To serve, pour a layer of pomegranate cordial on top of each portion of malabi (first mix this with a dash of pomegranate molasses if you want your syrup thicker or slightly less sweet). Sprinkle with the pistachios and grated coconut. Serve with an espresso – or, better still, Turkish coffee.

500 g (1 lb 2 oz) long red capsicums
    (bell peppers), stalks removed, left
    whole
2–4 green jalapeños, to taste (2 for mild,
    4 for hot), stalks removed, left whole
400 g (14 oz) mild feta-style cheese,
    made with cows' milk
55–80 g (2–2¾ oz/¼–⅓ cup) caster
    (superfine) sugar

EQUIPMENT
cook's blow-torch (available at
    kitchenware stores)

SPICY FETA BRÛLÉE

'It's not a recipe – it's an idea,' says chef Dan Zoaretz somewhat apologetically one Sunday morning as we stand in the empty kitchen of his restaurant, Dalida. In the dining room, the chairs have been placed upside down on the tables so that the cleaner can hoover up the tell-tale signs of the last feast of the weekend. I've asked Dan to show me how to make his signature spicy feta brûlée. The dish is admittedly somewhat light on ingredients – just four are needed, plus an oven, a food processor and a mini blow-torch. It's a neat counterpoint to the complicated fiddling of Michelin-starred chefs, recalling the punk bands whose three-minute songs, played with three chords and three instruments, stuck two fingers up at the symphonic excesses of the seventies.

This dish is the exception to the rule, in that it calls for the cheap, inauthentic feta-style cheese that's made with cow's milk (and therefore has a milder flavour) rather than real-deal Greek feta.

Preheat the oven to 250°C (480°F). Roast the capsicums and jalapeños in the oven for 25 minutes, turning them halfway through cooking. Set aside to cool, then purée first the capsicums then the jalapeños, seeds and all, in a food processor. Drain the capsicum purée in a fine-mesh sieve for 20 minutes or so.

Once drained, return the capsicums to the food processor and blend with the cheese to a smooth sauce. Blend in the jalapeño purée, a little at a time, tasting after each addition, until it is the right heat for you. Chill in the refrigerator for 3–4 hours to allow it to firm up.

Divide the cheese purée equally among six ramekins, smoothing the top of each with the back of a teaspoon and sprinkling with a single layer of sugar. Caramelise the sugar using the cook's blow-torch – or, in the absence of this handy tool, just under the red-hot grill (broiler) of your oven. Set aside to cool slightly before serving so that the sugar crust hardens.

Serve with a warm bread roll.

UM ALI

Chef Dan Zoaretz is a man of few words. That he named his restaurant after sixties' songstress Dalida has nothing to do with her most famous song, *Parole Parole*, and more to do with the fact that she was contradiction personified. The daughter of Italian emigrants, she grew up in Egypt, but shot to fame in France, and typical character traits from all three nationalities could be detected in her personality. Zoaretz, himself of Yemeni-Libyan origin, fuses European and Arabic cuisines in his restaurant. But there's more.

Displayed prominently at the front of the restaurant is a framed black-and-white photograph of the beautiful femme fatale. She's sitting on the pavement dressed in a chic pinstripe suit, looking into the camera lens with big, sensual eyes. You know the story: it's not going to end well. Dalida's short life was marked by commercial success, failed love affairs and drugs. One by one her exes committed suicide, and in the end she followed suit.

'Dalida's story is as colourful as it is tragic,' says Dan back in the kitchen. He's making me a version of the Egyptian dessert Um Ali, with a French twist. 'Dalida's unbalanced character inspires me in my cooking,' he continues. 'Some of the restaurant's dishes are very sophisticated and are made with more than ten ingredients. But we also serve simple pasta dishes. You can spend as much or as little money as you want to here.'

Zoaretz's elegant restaurant, in the heart of the charmingly chaotic Lewinsky district, is anything but vegetarian – its menu reveals a penchant for lamb and shellfish. But, just to show that it's possible, the chef's version of Um Ali is vegan. Literally translated, Um Ali means 'Ali's mother' and, coincidentally or not, while we make it, Dan's mother calls him. Twice.

Serves 12

CAKE
120 g (4½ oz) semolina
130 g (4½ oz) plain (all-purpose) flour
60 g (2 oz) ground almonds
160 g (5½ oz) sugar
1 × 8 g sachet baking powder
240 ml (8 fl oz) coconut cream
2 teaspoons olive oil, plus extra for greasing
1 tablespoon raw tahini
4 tablespoons rum (optional)

CREAM
35 g (1 oz/¼ cup) cornflour (cornstarch)
500 ml (17 fl oz/2 cups) rice milk
600 g (1 lb 5 oz) coconut cream
75 g (2¾ oz/⅓ cup) sugar

GARNISH
30 g (1 oz/¼ cup) raisins
2 tablespoons blanched almonds, lightly toasted
2 tablespoons pistachios, coarsely chopped

Preheat the oven to 180°C (350°F). Grease a high-sided 28 cm × 18 cm (11 in × 7 in) cake tin with simple olive oil and line with baking paper.

Mix all of the cake ingredients except the rum in a large bowl. Add 75 ml (2½ fl oz) of water and a pinch of salt. Beat with an electric mixer set to its lowest speed, until the cake batter is thick and smooth but still liquid. Pour the batter into the prepared tin and bake in the oven for 25 minutes, then set aside to cool before turning out onto a wire rack. Trim the edges of the cake: either use them to bribe your children to do their homework / tidy their room / give you a massage or eat them yourself. Cut the trimmed cake into 12 slices.

Fit each slice of cake into the bottom of a ramekin, glass or similar. Sprinkle a few of the raisins and almonds on top. At this stage, moisten each slice of cake with 1 teaspoon of rum (this is optional – it's my own delicious tweak to Dalida's original recipe).

For the cream, whisk the cornflour to a smooth paste with about half of the rice milk. Pour the remaining rice milk into a saucepan, add the coconut cream and sugar, and heat, stirring continuously, until the mixture is almost boiling. At this stage, add the cornflour mixture, reduce the heat, and continue to stir until the mixture is smooth and thickened enough to coat the back of a spoon. If it thickens too much, thin it out with a little more rice milk; if it's too thin, add more cornflour paste. Cover the contents of each ramekin with the cream mixture, then cover with plastic wrap and set aside to cool. Once cool, chill in the refrigerator.

Preheat the oven to 180°C (350°F). Arrange the ramekins on a baking tray and bake in the oven for 5 minutes. Garnish with the pistachios and the remaining almonds and raisins. Serve immediately, with a shot of rum alongside.

Serves 16

6 eggs, separated

150 g (5½ oz) cane sugar

75 ml (2½ fl oz) limoncello

grated zest of 1 large lemon

300 g (12½ oz/2 cups) almonds, skins on

230 g (8 oz/1½ cups) white chocolate,
  in pieces

200 g (7 oz) butter, plus extra for greasing

pinch of salt

30 g (1 oz/⅓ cup) flaked almonds

icing (confectioners') sugar for dusting

WHITE CHOCOLATE CAKE WITH ALMONDS AND LIMONCELLO

Restrictions stimulate creativity. This applies to all aspects of everyday life and particularly to the Passover kitchen (see page 313). Paradoxically, the ban on using seemingly indispensable baking ingredients such as flour and yeast actually makes Passover pastries the culinary highlight of the Jewish year. This cake is the proof. Besides being kosher for Passover, it's also completely gluten free.

Preheat the oven to 180°C (350°F). Grease a 24 cm (9½ in) springform cake tin with butter.

Using an electric mixer, whisk the egg yolks in a large, grease-free bowl with about half of the sugar and all of the limoncello and lemon zest, until the mixture is pale and thick. Set aside.

Toast the almonds in a dry frying pan until lightly scorched, then transfer them to the bowl of a food processor and grind with the white chocolate until the mixture has the consistency of breadcrumbs. Melt the butter in a small saucepan over medium heat, then pour it over the chocolate-almond mixture and blitz again. Set aside.

Using your electric mixer, whisk the egg whites with the remaining sugar and a pinch of salt in a grease-free mixing bowl (make sure that the whisks are also squeaky clean). Keep going until stiff peaks form – they need to be as stiff as possible, with the consistency of shaving foam.

Fold the chocolate-almond mixture into the egg-yolk mixture until well combined. Then, carefully fold in the egg-white mixture. This may seem like mission impossible due to the vastly different consistencies of the two mixtures, but carry on carefully and patiently and eventually you'll have a smooth, airy cake batter. (Don't be alarmed by the loss of volume.)

Scrape the batter into the prepared cake tin. Bake in the oven for 40 minutes, or until it tests done with a skewer – if the skewer inserted into the centre of the cake comes out clean, the cake is cooked. Set aside to cool completely in the tin, then remove the springform mould.

To finish, toast the flaked almonds in a dry frying pan until golden brown. Dust the cooled cake with icing sugar and sprinkle with the toasted almond flakes. Keep the cake, covered, in the refrigerator, and serve chilled.

SLOW-COOKED BEEF STEW WITH SWEET POTATOES, GREMOLATA AND TAHINI

This is an ideal dish to make in advance at home, in preparation for a weekend in a self-catering cottage with the family; I made it for our annual trip to the Dutch version of Disneyland. My in-laws loved it, but I couldn't get over my disappointment – I had left the magic ingredient, the tahini, at home on the kitchen bench by mistake. There was no opportunity for a do-over: the following year when my family visited the theme park for the weekend, I was working on this book in Tel Aviv. It was for the best for everyone involved.

Preheat the oven to 110°C (230°F).

Heat the fat in a heavy-based (ideally cast-iron), ovenproof saucepan over high heat. Brown the meat in batches, then transfer to a plate. Reduce the heat and fry the onions and garlic for 4–5 minutes, until softened. Stir in the flour and continue to cook, stirring well, until the onions brown. Return the meat to the pan with 200 ml (7 fl oz) water, the salt, wine, stock cubes and vinegar. Stir well to deglaze the bottom of the pan.

Using cooking string, tie the thyme, rosemary and bay leaves tightly around the cloves; push the herbs down into the stew. Bring the mixture to the boil, then transfer the pan to the oven and cook for 4–5 hours, reducing the temperature to 100°C (210°F) after 1 hour. Check on the stew every hour or so, adding boiling water if it seems a little dry. The stew is cooked when the meat is fall-apart tender – remove it from the oven, discard the herb bundle and set it aside to cool. Chill in the refrigerator overnight (this will make the meat even more tender).

An hour before serving the stew, preheat the oven to 190°C (375°F). Prick holes in the sweet potatoes using a fork, then rub them all over with the oil. Wrap each sweet potato in foil and roast in the oven for 1 hour, or until tender. Meanwhile, heat the stew through over low heat and season with salt and freshly ground black pepper.

Meanwhile, for the gremolata, blitz the lemon zest, garlic and parsley in a food processor until finely chopped. Gradually stir in extra virgin olive oil in a thin stream, until the sauce has the consistency of pesto. Season to taste with salt and freshly ground black pepper.

To serve, unwrap the sweet potatoes and cut each in half. Place 2 sweet-potato halves onto each plate. Spoon over the stew and drizzle with the tahini and gremolata.

Serves 8

2 × quantities tahini (page 282)
2 tablespoons schmaltz (page 308) or olive oil

1.5 kg (3 lb 5 oz) stewing beef (such as braising steak), cut into large cubes
5 large onions, coarsely chopped
4 garlic cloves, sliced
50 g (1¾ oz/⅓ cup) plain (all-purpose) flour
pinch of salt
150 ml (5 fl oz) red wine
2 beef stock (bouillon) cubes
2 tablespoons wine vinegar
½ bunch of thyme
½ bunch of rosemary
4 bay leaves
5 cloves
8 orange sweet potatoes (about 150–200 g/5½–7 oz each), scrubbed
extra virgin olive oil

GREMOLATA
grated zest of 1 lemon
1 garlic clove, crushed
1 bunch of flat-leaf (Italian) parsley
extra virgin olive oil
salt and freshly ground black pepper

SALATIM

Weekend brunch in Ha'achiem

Serves 4

2 large eggplants (aubergines)
3 tablespoons raw tahini
1 tablespoon lemon juice
1 roasted garlic clove (page 286),
　　or 1 raw garlic clove, crushed
salt and freshly ground black pepper
extra virgin olive oil

Blacken the eggplants over the open flame of your hob or, if you do not have a gas cooker, under the grill (broiler) (see instructions on page 299). Set the eggplants aside to cool slightly. Holding the eggplants over a bowl, carefully peel off the blackened skin, catching any juice from the cooked eggplants in the bowl.

Mix the raw tahini, lemon juice and roasted garlic to a stiff paste in a large bowl.

Mash the eggplant flesh into the tahini mixture; loosen with the reserved eggplant juice if necessary. Season to taste with plenty of salt and freshly ground black pepper, and a generous dash of good-quality olive oil.

Serve the baba ghanoush sprinkled with your choice of garnish, such as thinly sliced green chilli, thinly sliced spring onion and nigella seeds, or pomegranate seeds and chopped mint leaves.

BABA GHANOUSH (SALAT CHATZILIM)

Baba ghanoush is, next to hummus and tahini, one of The Big Three in Israeli cuisine, thought of as dips or sauces outside of Israel, but considered salads by Israelis. They're incomparably delicious when made from scratch, but don't kid yourself – most Israelis buy these beloved staples ready made. The range offered in supermarkets is almost inexhaustible, although there are only marginal differences between the rows of plastic containers. Steer well clear of crazy flavours and unusual colours – keep in mind the refrain of the well-known Dutch food writer Johannes van Dam, who said that variety is a symptom of ignorance. The more fundamental a dish is to a people, the simpler it is to make.

In Israel, baba ghanoush consists of nothing more than roasted eggplant and tahini (or, when needs must, mayonnaise). It may well have a colourful garnish, but this is never over-the-top – by contrast, most European cookbooks suggest a carnival procession of nuts, seeds, leaves and spices to garnish their baba ghanoush, all of which only serve to mask the unique smoky flavour of the eggplant. Incidentally, Israelis hardly ever call the dish 'baba ghanoush' (or by its other name, *mutabal*); they refer to it as *salat chatzilim* ('eggplant salad') or, depending on the preparation, *chatzil ba'tahini* or *chatzil ba'mayonnaise*. The best version, as far as I'm concerned, is homemade baba ghanoush made with tahini.

The Arab hummus Abu Hassan in Jaffo serves according to many the best hummus of Tel Aviv. There are always long queues at the weekend.

NO MORE FACTORY SLURRIES

In the sweltering summer of 2003, an Israeli eatery serving nothing but hummus opened its doors on a New York street somewhere between Avenue A and First Avenue. I had just moved into a spacious-for-Manhattan apartment three blocks away, the size of not one, but two wardrobes. There I lived in utter bliss with my newlywed wife and a belligerent army of cockroaches who would march about in formation at the most inconvenient moments – at night, for example, when my head was blocking their route across my pillow.

They were good times. My wife was working in a hospital on First Avenue and I appointed myself CEO – Chief Eating Officer. My mission was to find out about new restaurants opening in the city before the whole of hip New York descended on them, thereby making getting a reservation without the necessary connections all but impossible. So it was that, on a Sunday afternoon, we took our seats at a pavement table outside this brand-new hummus restaurant.

We had both once lived in Israel for a year and had eaten hummus three times a day, every day – but neither of us had ever tasted the dish freshly made. We tucked in eagerly. What a disappointment! The hummus had no flavour and had a curious consistency that was nothing like the delicious mass-produced hummus that we remembered from our year in Israel. We both agreed that this place would last less than six months. On the way home, we bought a packet of supermarket hummus and some bread, which we ate defiantly on a bench in Tompkins Square Park.

I don't know if that restaurant still exists, and have no idea what the quality of their hummus was actually like, in retrospect. What I know now is that it took me years to get used to hummus made without artificial flavourings and preservatives. If you don't know any better, you cleave automatically to what you know, and this product – however poor-quality – becomes the standard by which you measure everything else. It's like drinking instant coffee all your life and then not being able to stomach espresso made from freshly ground arabica beans.

Nowadays, of course, I can't even look at supermarket hummus. When I am overcome by a longing for hummus, I cycle to Amsterdam's D & A Hummus Bistro, where they serve exceptionally good, freshly made hummus.

It is possible and not at all difficult to make hummus yourself. There are only two obstacles. Firstly, you have to know today that tomorrow you're going to be in the mood for hummus, because you have to make real hummus with dried chickpeas that have been soaked overnight. Secondly, you have to wean yourself off that damn factory slurry – and this feat can't often be accomplished overnight.

HUMMUS

There are so very many bad recipes for hummus in circulation. I regularly come across shamefully bad versions – not just on food blogs, but also on renowned cookery programs and in highly respected cookbooks. It doesn't help that – here in the Netherlands at least – most people have no idea how hummus should actually taste. Ninety-nine percent of the time, the nasty spreads to which cafés and restaurants subject their oblivious clientèle bear absolutely no resemblance to the divine dip you'll find on every street corner in Tel Aviv.

For a long time, Dutch businesses could use the excuse of not knowing any better. You could order authentic hummus in the odd Lebanese restaurant, but restaurants specialising in hummus just didn't exist. Now, there are several in Amsterdam alone, operated by Israeli ex-pats who saw a gap in the market for the hummus from their homeland. Find one where you live and go and taste hummus there – not in a sandwich with roasted vegetables, but served as a dish in itself. Good-quality, freshly made hummus needs only a dash of olive oil, a pinch of paprika and a sprinkling of chopped parsley – plus torn pieces of warm pitta with which to scoop it up (no cutlery needed).

If you're used to the flavour of genuine hummus, there's nothing else standing in the way of you making your own. The quality of the tahini you use is essential, since the secret of Israeli hummus is a ridiculous amount of tahini – we're talking half a jar, rather than the two measly tablespoons recommended in most bad recipes. If possible, buy Israeli, Palestinian or Lebanese tahini, and avoid Turkish or Greek brands (which work better in Turkish and Greek dishes).

Despite being an inspired combination of only four main ingredients, plus some water and salt, hummus is a tricky dish to get right – there's no room for complacency or frivolity. Never use tinned chickpeas. Hummus made with tinned chickpeas won't look any different – a mush is a mush is a mush – but the difference in flavour and texture will be huge. Besides, soaking the dried chickpeas isn't actually any effort – you just have to plan ahead the night before you want to eat hummus.

Before you get started, some tips and tricks. Firstly, buy the smallest chickpeas you can find, as they're usually the tastiest. Secondly, resist the temptation to liven up your hummus with spices such as cumin – when it comes to hummus, less is most definitely more. Lastly, don't make the classic mistake of cutting your hummus with olive oil – unsurprisingly, the structure will be oily rather than creamy. Save your olive oil and instead use it to garnish your freshly prepared hummus.

Serves 6

2 teaspoons baking soda
    (bicarbonate of soda)
250 g (9 oz) dried chickpeas
2 garlic cloves, crushed
225 g (8 oz) raw tahini
juice of 1–1½ lemons
1 teaspoon salt
1 flat-leaf (Italian) parsley sprig,
    leaves finely chopped
pinch of paprika

Dissolve 1 teaspoon of the bicarbonate of soda in a large bowl of cold water and soak the chickpeas for at least 12 hours. Drain and rinse the soaked chickpeas under cold running water, then dissolve the remaining teaspoon of baking soda in a large, lidded saucepan of water, add the chickpeas and bring to the boil. There should be about 3 cm (1¼ in) of water covering the chickpeas. When the water is boiling, cover the pan with the lid and reduce the heat until the water is simmering. Simmer for at least 45 minutes, or even double that, depending on your chickpeas – they are done when they start to fall apart. Halfway through cooking, remove 1 tablespoon of al dente chickpeas from the pan and reserve for the garnish.

Drain the cooked chickpeas in a colander suspended over a bowl, collecting the cooking liquid in the bowl. Set the drained chickpeas aside to cool slightly, then blend them in a food processor with the garlic, raw tahini and the juice of 1 lemon. Keep the motor running for at least 10 minutes, adding a splash of the cooking liquid now and then to loosen the mixture if it becomes too sticky; keep the mixture quite thick at this stage, however.

Season the hummus to taste, with up to 1 teaspoon of salt and maybe a touch more lemon juice. It's crucial to keep tasting the hummus as you season it! When you're completely satisfied, dilute the hummus to the desired consistency using a little more of the reserved cooking liquid.

If you're not serving the hummus right away, cover it and chill in the refrigerator until needed; before serving, taste and season once more with salt and lemon juice, and loosen again with a splash more cooking liquid, if necessary.

To serve, spread a large dollop of hummus all over a plate using the back of a spoon. Make a well in the middle by holding the spoon still and turning the plate. Spoon the reserved chickpeas into the well, and pour in enough olive oil to fill it. (If you forgot to reserve any chickpeas, tinned chickpeas will do for the garnish.) Sprinkle with the parsley and paprika.

HUMMUS WITH PULLED CHICKEN

Serves 4–6

½ × quantity hummus (page 236)

simple olive oil for frying
1 large onion, grated
2 garlic cloves, coarsely chopped
½ teaspoon ground coriander
½ teaspoon ground cumin
½ teaspoon ground cinnamon
½ teaspoon ground turmeric
½ teaspoon ground mace
½ teaspoon paprika
1 teaspoon curry powder
2 teaspoons harissa
2 teaspoons tomato paste
   (concentrated purée)
3 tablespoons white wine vinegar
2 teaspoons silan or date syrup
2 chicken leg quarters (about 350 g/
   12½ oz total weight)
salt to season

TO SERVE
4–6 pittas
handful of pine nuts, toasted
4 flat-leaf (Italian) parsley sprigs,
   leaves coarsely chopped
extra virgin olive oil
pinch of paprika

Freshly made hummus doesn't need any frills. Still, if I want to impress my guests – and that is always the case – plain hummus just won't do. When it comes to cooking, I recognise myself in the line of The Kinks' *Dedicated Follower of Fashion*: 'There's one thing that he loves and that is flattery.' This topping of hot and spicy slow-cooked chicken is guaranteed to achieve the desired effect. Make sure you make plenty of chicken, because everyone will want a second helping.

Heat a good dash of olive oil in a heavy-based, lidded saucepan just large enough to fit the two chicken leg quarters next to each other. Fry the onion and garlic over medium heat for 3–4 minutes, until softened, then stir in the spices, curry powder, harissa, tomato paste, vinegar, silan and 100 ml (3½ fl oz) of water to make a smooth paste. Add the chicken leg quarters, stirring to coat them in the sauce, cover the pan with the lid, reduce the heat to its lowest setting and braise for 1 hour, turning the meat halfway through cooking.

When the chicken is cooked through (no trace of pink remains when pierced at the thickest part of the thigh), remove it from the sauce and set it aside to cool. When cool enough to handle, pick the meat from the bones. Pull any larger pieces of chicken apart. Return the meat to the pan and cook for a few minutes longer, until the chicken is warmed through and the sauce has thickened slightly. Season to taste with salt.

Half an hour before you want to eat, remove the hummus from the refrigerator so that it can come up to room temperature.

To serve, warm the pittas briefly in a toaster. Spoon 3–4 heaped tablespoons of hummus into the centre of each plate, spreading them around the plate with the bottom of the spoon. Make a well in the centre of the hummus and fill with the warm pulled chicken. Garnish with the pine nuts, parsley, extra virgin olive oil and a pinch of paprika. Serve the pittas alongside.

½ × quantity hummus (page 236)
1 teaspoon TLV spice mix (page 288) or
    ras el hanout/baharat

3 tablespoons pistachios
dash of simple olive oil
1 garlic clove, finely chopped
½ teaspoon ground coriander
½ teaspoon ground cumin
½ teaspoon ground cinnamon
1 teaspoon harissa
400 g (14 oz) minced (ground) beef
3 spring onions (scallions), trimmed and
    sliced into rings
3 tablespoons pomegranate seeds
salt
4–6 pittas
4 mint sprigs, leaves coarsely chopped
extra virgin olive oil to garnish

HUMMUS WITH MINCED BEEF AND POMEGRANATES

Hummus is incredibly versatile. That statement doesn't extend to sweet toppings, but just about every savoury topping you can think of works really well with it. Spoon leftovers from last night's dinner – goulash, pasta sauce, ragout, whatever – over a plate of hummus and you'll probably enjoy it more than you did the original meal.

Because a recipe for scraps is a contradiction in terms, here's my quick version of *hummus im basar* ('hummus with meat'). Instead of the tried-and-tested combination of minced beef with pine nuts and parsley, I garnish my meat with pistachios, mint and pomegranate seeds. The pomegranate seeds are not – as is so often the case – just there to add colour; their pleasant sweet-sour tang is a great foil to the spiced meat. An unexpected bonus of serving pomegranate seeds warm is that all of a sudden the bitter white fibres that usually embed themselves between your teeth are hardly noticeable.

Be sensible and make just a little more of this dish than you actually need. Then you'll have something to look forward to tomorrow.

Lightly toast the pistachios in a dry frying pan, or on a baking tray in an oven preheated to 180°C (350°F). Set aside to cool, then chop coarsely.

Heat a dash of olive oil in a frying pan, add the garlic and spices and stir-fry for a few seconds until aromatic. Add the minced beef and stir-fry, breaking down any clumps of meat with a wooden spoon. When the beef is browned on the outside but not cooked through, add the spring onions. Continue to stir-fry until the beef is just cooked through, then stir through the pomegranate seeds and pistachios (don't add them too early or the pomegranate seeds will discolour and the pistachios will lose their crunch). Remove the pan from the heat and season to taste with salt.

Half an hour before you want to eat, remove the hummus from the refrigerator so that it can come up to room temperature. To serve, warm the pittas briefly in a toaster. Spoon 3–4 heaped tablespoons of hummus into the centre of each plate, spreading them around the plate with the bottom of the spoon. Make a well in the centre of the hummus and fill with the minced beef mixture. Garnish with the mint leaves and drizzle with a dash of extra virgin olive oil. Serve the pittas alongside.

ASHKENAZI VS. SEPHARDIC

It was a close call, but my promising young life might have been cut short at a mere seventeen summers in the surf of the Mediterranean. My Jewish youth club's trip to Israel was over, but I was staying in the country for another week – something I was very excited about, since I'd never been on holiday alone before. After waving my friends off at the airport, I got on a bus to Tel Aviv. It was early morning when I arrived; the city was still asleep. Since everything was closed, I decided to go swimming in the sea.

I was not alone in the sea: a dark-skinned man in his fifties, with enough white chest hair to knit himself a winter sweater, was swimming my way. If there are just two of you in the sea, you can't really ignore each other. After four weeks of Israeli sun, I must have looked like a native, because the man immediately started talking to me in quick, unimpregnable Hebrew. While he stood talking to me, feet comfortably planted on the seabed, I was awkwardly treading water. When I explained that I was a Dutch tourist, he searched for alternative common ground: was I Sephardic? The answer to this question is no, because even though my mother has Spanish–Portuguese Jewish ancestry, and is therefore Sephardic, I was brought up with the Ashkenazi rituals of my father. The man waited for me to answer with an expectant smile. '*Has vehalila!*' ('God forbid!') I joked, thinking of the Sephardic branch of my family. The man's cheerful expression vanished and he started to yell at me. Although I couldn't understand what he was shouting, I did immediately understand that I was in danger. I tried to swim away, but he grabbed my foot and pulled me under the water. If the karate kick I sent his way with my other foot hadn't landed him squarely in the balls, I probably wouldn't have lived to tell this tale.

I didn't understand what had happened. During our youth club trip, no one had mentioned the harrowing oppression of Sephardic Jews. How was I to know that they were treated as foreigners by Israeli society? That all positions of influence and importance were taken by Ashkenazi Jews?

The terms 'Ashkenazi' and 'Sephardic' date to medieval times, when two large Jewish communities lived separately from each other in what is now Europe: the Jews in the south were called *Sephardim* ('Spaniards') while those in the east were *Ashkenazim* ('Germans'). Over the centuries, these communities, both influenced by their non-Jewish environment, developed different customs, rituals and dishes. However, in Israeli society, this distinction is not what defines citizens as either Ashkenazi or Sephardic. Since the arrival of the first pioneers in the late nineteenth century, Israel has been split along socio-economic lines: a privileged class made up of Jews from Christian countries, and an underclass comprising Jews from Muslim countries. So, although etymologically inaccurate, in Israel, Jews with Moroccan, Tunisian, Iraqi, Iranian or Yemeni heritage are known as *Sephardim*, while those with ancestors from Europe, the United States or Latin America call themselves *Ashkenazim*.

It is striking that Israel, the first Western democracy to elect a female prime minister, is still waiting for its first Sephardic prime minister, when more than half of the Jewish population is Sephardic. The legacy of the once grinding (now much improved) deprivation suffered by Israel's Sephardic Jews is evident in the country's culinary divide: traditionally, street food was mainly Sephardic in origin, whereas restaurant menus were European through and through. This distinction has largely disappeared in recent years: Israeli cooks have come to realise that the average Israeli doesn't want (or can't afford) to eat French-style dishes. Luxury restaurants have given way to a flourishing scene of informal mid-range restaurants in which Sephardic smells and flavours dominate. The result? Israelis have never eaten as well as they do today.

If I ever again meet anyone in the Tel Aviv waves who asks me whether I'm Sephardic, my answer will be: '*Halevai!*' ('I wish!').

ROASTED CAPSICUMS WITH GOAT'S CHEESE AND PINE NUTS

Serves 4

It always amazes me how much capsicums improve by being set on fire: the flames transform this watery, wishy-washy vegetable into the radiant star of an awesome salad.

2 red or yellow capsicums (bell peppers)
3 tablespoons olive oil
1 tablespoon red wine vinegar
1 tablespoon pomegranate molasses
salt and freshly ground black pepper
30 g (1 oz/¾ cup) rocket (arugula)
100 g (3½ oz) soft goat's cheese, crumbled
3 tablespoons pine nuts, toasted
1 tablespoon good-quality balsamic vinegar

Blacken the capsicums over the open flame of your hob or, if you don't have a gas stove, under the grill (broiler) (see instructions on page 298). Once completely blackened, seal in zip-lock bags and set aside to cool. When cool, peel the capsicums, remove the stalks and seeds, and slice the flesh into long, thin strips.

Meanwhile, in a bowl, whisk the olive oil, vinegar and molasses until well combined (don't worry if the mixture is a bit lumpy). Season to taste with salt and freshly ground black pepper, bearing in mind that the goat's cheese will be salty. Marinate the capsicum strips in this dressing until ready to serve.

To serve, make a bed of rocket on each of four plates and spoon the capsicum strips, and their dressing, on top. Sprinkle over the crumbled goat's cheese and toasted pine nuts. Hold the tablespoon of balsamic vinegar in your left hand (if you're right-handed) and use the point of a knife to spatter a nice pattern over each serving. Serve immediately.

schmaltz (page 308) or sunflower oil

1 × 600 g (1 lb 5 oz) piece of fat-
    marbled skirt steak
8 radishes, sliced
1 ripe plum, pitted and sliced
1 red onion, roughly chopped
1 green chilli, deseeded (if desired),
    sliced into rings
4 spring onions (scallions), green
    part only, sliced
15 g (½ oz/¼ cup) flat-leaf (Italian)
    parsley, roughly chopped
15 g (½ oz/¼ cup) celery tops,
    roughly chopped
15 g (½ oz/¼ cup) basil, roughly
    chopped
juice of 1 lemon (to taste)
a few glugs of extra virgin olive oil
salt and freshly ground black pepper

Remove the meat from the refrigerator
and let it come up to room temperature,
then rub it all over with the fat. Set aside.

Mix together all of the remaining
ingredients, apart from the lemon juice
and olive oil, in a large bowl. Stir in the
lemon juice, to taste, then add about
twice as much olive oil and toss well.

Heat a large, heavy-based frying pan
over high heat until smoking hot. Using
a stopwatch, fry the meat for exactly
60 seconds per side. Reduce the heat to
medium, then cook the meat for another
60 seconds on each side. (In total, the
meat is cooked for 4 minutes.)

Remove the meat from the pan and carve
it against the grain into thin slices using
a sharp knife. Add the meat to the salad,
along with any meat juices from the pan.
Season to taste with salt and freshly
ground black pepper.

To serve, divide the salad equally among
four plates and enjoy with a fruity red wine.

SALAD OF FLASH-FRIED BEEF, PLUM AND HERBS

In a nondescript alley that divides two lively thoroughfares of Tel Aviv's Carmel Market you'll find what is perhaps the best meat restaurant in the city. It doesn't look that way from the outside: like all eateries in this part of town, M25 blends in with its market surroundings (see pictures on pages 136–143). In front of the concrete building – once the workshop of a market stall – are some picnic tables. Those who prefer not to eat amid the roar of trucks and the detritus of discarded fruit crates can sit inside, where the dining area is separated from the open kitchen by a butcher's display cabinet, allowing diners to choose their own piece of meat. There are strip lights on the ceiling, abattoir tiles on the floor, and fans working overtime on the walls. There's no menu; instead, all the options are chalked up on a large blackboard.

M25's name refers to its dedicated butchers, located in the same market some 25 metres further up. You can order outstanding steaks from the staff, who are clad in striped butchers' aprons, but if you're feeling adventurous, plump for the shakshuka with calf brains. Or for the slow-cooked beef heart. Or else for one of the Ashkenazi classics that have been given a new lease of life by chef-patron Jonathan Borowitz. His chopped liver, for example, swaps chicken livers for lamb's liver, and is imbued with creaminess through the addition of lamb brains.

Jonathan was enthusiastic when I asked him to contribute a recipe to this book, but we had difficulty coming up with a recipe that honoured the spirit of M25 but could be successfully brought to the table by home cooks without any butchery training. In the end, we chose this salad. At M25, it's made with veal sweetbreads from M25's own smokehouse, but this more accessible version, which uses skirt steak, was prepared for me by the chef himself, and is not to be sneezed at.

HUSSAR'S SALAD

Serves 6

600 g (1 lb 5 oz) left-over cooked smoked
    tongue (page 141), diced, or (800 g/
    1 lb 12 oz) stewing beef

3 boiling potatoes, peeled
1 onion, finely chopped
1 granny smith (or similar tart green
    apple), peeled, cored, diced
3 gherkins (pickles), diced
2 boiled beetroot (beets), diced
1–2 tablespoons mayonnaise
1–2 tablespoons left-over mustard-thyme
    vinaigrette (optional; page 141)
salt and freshly ground black pepper

This recipe is an upgrade of my mother's Hussar's salad, who in turn got it from her father, my grandfather Maurits. I've replaced the stewing beef they used with the left-over meat from my recipe for smoked beef tongue with beetroot and quail eggs (page 141). Neither my version of the salad nor my mother's even remotely resembles the sludgy factory-produced 'Russian salad' sold by convenience stores – for one thing, ours is deep purple in colour, unlike the light-grey or beige hues of the mass-produced stuff. I was curious as to how our dish has been passed off as Hussar's salad for generations. My mother has no idea, and grandfather Maurits has been dead for twenty years.

I'm not sure of my case, but I have a theory. With my detective's hat on, I scrolled through the unending stream of images that, according to Google, corresponded to the search term 'Hussar's salad'. This is a popular Dutch classic, often served on New Year's Eve and at other celebrations, and everyone has their own way of presenting it. All the clichés slid up the screen past my eyes: tomatoes fashioned into roses, stuffed eggs, fanned gherkin slices and sprigs of curly parsley. What they all masked was the same grey mound of salad.

I was just about to get an attack of 'smartphone thumb', when suddenly I scrolled past a purple salad. According to the caption, it came from Suriname, and I'll be damned: if the search term 'Surinamese Hussar's salad' didn't turn my whole screen beetroot purple.

This is my hypothesis: my mother's branch of the family tree stems from Spanish-Portuguese Jews who fled the infernal regime of the royal couple Ferdinand and Isabella (of Inquisition fame) at the end of the 15ᵗʰ century. A great number of her relatives ended up in Amsterdam; after a few detours, other members of the family settled in Suriname. My lovely Aunt Irma was one such Surinamese-Jewish woman – what I remember most about her are her thick accent and her large size. She was a good friend of my grandparents, so it's possible that my grandfather's Hussar's salad recipe came from her. I'll never know for sure: Aunt Irma is no longer here to confirm or deny it – she died in 2017 at a ripe old age.

If you're not using left-over cooked tongue meat, then simmer the stewing beef with a beef stock (bouillon) cube and a bay leaf in 1 litre (34 fl oz/4 cups) of water for 3 hours. Drain, set aside to cool completely, then dice.

In a separate saucepan, boil the potatoes in salted water until tender (but not falling apart); drain and set aside to cool. Once completely cooled, cut into dice.

Mix the meat, potatoes and the remaining fruit and vegetables together in a large bowl, then stir through the mayonnaise (and a little of the left-over mustard-thyme vinaigrette, if desired). Season to taste with salt and freshly ground black pepper.

Before serving, chill in the refrigerator for 1–2 hours to allow the flavours to develop.

Serves 4

40 g (1½ oz/¼ cup) sesame seeds
8 ripe tomatoes, cut into small cubes
4 Lebanese (short) cucumbers, cut into
    small cubes
1 Romano pepper (capsicum), cut into
    small cubes
1 small red onion, thinly sliced into
    half-moon shapes
75 g (2¾ oz) pitted kalamata olives,
    thinly sliced
½ bunch of radishes, trimmed and
    thinly sliced
½ bunch of flat-leaf (Italian) parsley,
    finely chopped
juice of ½ lemon
extra virgin olive oil
salt and freshly ground black pepper
200 g (7 oz) cottage cheese
2 tablespoons za'atar

Dry-fry the sesame seeds until toasted
a pale golden brown. Do not take
your eyes off the seeds as they cook,
because they will burn quickly. Transfer
to a bowl and set aside to cool.

Toss the tomatoes, cucumbers,
capsicum, onion, olives, radishes and
parsley in a large serving bowl with the
lemon juice and a generous splash of
olive oil. Season with salt and freshly
ground black pepper.

Top the salad with the cottage cheese
and sprinkle over the za'atar and
toasted sesame seeds. Drizzle with a
little more olive oil and serve.

ISRAELI SALAD WITH COTTAGE CHEESE AND ZA'ATAR

Tel Aviv is a paradise for vegetarians. The city has stacks of meat- and fish-free eateries, but even in regular restaurants there are invariably plenty of vegetable-only dishes on the menu. Not sissy side dishes purely there to ease the chef's conscience, either, but signature dishes from chefs who want to boast of the country's awesome vegetables.

At breakfast and lunch, Israeli salad is served as standard. At its most austere, this might be no more than a few cubes of tomato and cucumber, a shredded onion and some finely chopped parsley. More elaborate versions will be supplemented with fresh herbs such as mint and coriander (cilantro) and any vegetables that can conceivably be eaten raw: capsicums (bell peppers), spring onions (scallions), radishes, carrots, fennel, chillies, olives ... The only rule is that they must be finely chopped. *Dak-dak*, as the Israelis say. The dressing is as simple as it is unbeatable: good-quality olive oil, freshly squeezed lemon juice, a pinch of salt and a grinding of freshly ground black pepper. A dish of tahini is never far from reach.

Like many of the country's national dishes, Israeli salad has Arabic roots. The label 'Israeli' is mainly used by nationalists, travel guides, foreign food writers and the Ministry of Tourism. Most restaurants in left-wing Tel Aviv simply call it 'Arabic salad' or 'vegetable salad'. Add a wide range of fresh, creamy cheeses to your salad and you've got yourself an Israeli breakfast (a term that no one disputes). Eat it with a glass of freshly squeezed orange juice, a cappuccino and possibly a fried egg, and you'll be set up for the day.

LABNEH WITH PISTACHIO, POMEGRANATE, SOY AND SILAN

When mingling in gastronomic circles, I sometimes experience a classic Babylonian confusion of tongues. When I speak about hummus, I pronounce it the Hebrew way, which confuses my Dutch friends; when I boast about my homemade *labaneh*, I hit a similar wall of incomprehension. 'Oh, you mean *l-e-bneh!*' people say snootily once they've cottoned on, visibly stunned by my shameless display of ignorance.

Of course I know what I'm talking about. Like any card-carrying foodie, I'd have had to have been living under a rock to not have heard of this hip do-it-yourself strained yoghurt. It's still not for sale in the supermarkets where I live, but it's easy to make yourself. All you need is a tub of goat's-milk yoghurt, a piece of muslin, a pinch of salt and a generous helping of patience.

As has often been the case in recent years, this much-hyped culinary trend originates from the Middle East. Its roots are unquestionably Arabic, which is why those in the know pronounce it with an Arabic accent ('lebneh'). In Israel, where it's just as popular, labneh is known as *labaneh*. In both Arabic and Hebrew, the word for labneh has at its root the word 'white'. I'm not arguing with this etymology, but it doesn't make things any easier when you're standing in the dairy aisle.

Labneh is sometimes translated as 'curd cheese', a name that refers to the process of making it. And actually, it's not so new and hip. People from our grandmothers' generation made it, but stopped as soon as factory-produced cheese rendered all that fiddling with muslin redundant. Nevertheless, labneh and curd cheese are not quite the same thing.

In the Netherlands at least, curd cheese is sold in the bigger supermarkets, but it's made from cow's milk and is therefore not thick and luscious enough to be used as a substitute for labneh. So we just roll up our sleeves and make some ourselves. Choose goat's-milk yoghurt that's at least three percent fat: by straining this yoghurt, the whey (liquid) separates from the solid curd.

If you don't have a piece of muslin, feel free to strain the yoghurt through a thin, clean tea towel. In a pinch, use a clean pair of your girlfriend's tights – but only if you're really in love.

Serves 2–4

500 g (1 lb 2 oz/2 cups) full-fat goat's-milk yoghurt (3.5% fat or above)
500 g (1 lb 2 oz/2 cups) Turkish yoghurt (10% fat or above)
1 teaspoon salt
handful of pistachios
handful of pomegranate seeds
1 mint sprig, leaves chopped
extra virgin olive oil
silan or date syrup
1 teaspoon sumac
2–4 laffa (page 300) or pittas

Line a bowl with a piece of muslin (cheesecloth), add both types of yoghurt and mix in the salt. Bring the edges of the muslin together and tie tightly with cooking string to form a pouch. Hang this pouch in the refrigerator somehow (I tie it to the metal drinks rack), still suspended over the bowl to catch the strained liquid. (If you can't make this work, then place the pouch into a fine-mesh sieve and suspend that over the bowl – this takes more time, but it should be ready after 24 hours in the refrigerator.)

When the yoghurt has strained, toast the pistachios in a dry frying pan, transfer them to a bowl to cool, then chop roughly.

To serve, spread about half of the labneh onto a large sharing plate using the bottom of a spoon (the remaining labneh can be kept in the refrigerator for a few days, for use in another recipe – see page 259). Sprinkle over the pistachios, pomegranate seeds and chopped mint leaves and drizzle with olive oil and silan. Finish with a few pinches of the sumac.

Serve with the laffa or pittas.

THE TASTE OF SURVIVAL

It's Tuesday morning. As usual, Eyal Shani parks his car in front of the barrier at the start of the gravel path that provides access from the Arab town of Abu Ghosh to the green hills west of Jerusalem. On the horizon, encased in a layer of smog, the silhouette of Tel Aviv, where Shani runs eight leading restaurants, is still just visible.

Shani is much in demand and usually concentrates exclusively on his restaurants, but he made an exception for me when I asked him to appear in my television series, *The Kosher Dilemma*. The subject of this episode is za'atar, a herb that grows in and around Israel but is remarkably difficult to find in its fresh form. All za'atar, it seems, ends up dried in spice blends, along with sesame seeds and ground sumac, a sour dried berry. But Eyal Shani is not one for dried herbs and spices. The strong-willed chef uses only fresh herbs in his restaurants, preferably picked himself. And on this hot summer's day, I'm allowed to go along with him.

'This is my back garden,' says the top chef, as he makes Turkish coffee on a gas stove from the boot of his car. Apart from my cameraman and director, there's not a soul around. 'I've been coming here every week for twenty-five years to visit my friends.' Shani's friends turn out to be the herbs. 'I talk to them,' he says. 'I can tell how they're feeling. Because I've built up a relationship of trust with them, I can cook with them.' He tells me all this with a completely straight face, and coming from him it all sounds completely logical.

All around us, under the still-blazing October sun, bushy sage plants are waving their branches in the breeze – but it takes us a while to find any za'atar. It's not really the season, because the plant can't easily withstand the scorching heat of summer. 'But now is exactly when it tastes at its best,' says Shani, uprooting a few dry branches of za'atar. 'This is the ultimate taste of Israel,' the chef philosophises. 'It's the taste of survival.'

That picking wild za'atar is against the law doesn't worry Shani. Yes, he's been arrested by special patrols on occasion, but most of the time the wardens leave him alone rather than risk a confrontation with the smooth-talking celebrity chef. Wild za'atar might be at risk of extinction, but Shani remains sanguine about his actions. 'As long as you pick za'atar for your own happiness and not to make money from it, then you have a right to do so.' 'But,' I protest, 'you serve the za'atar in your restaurants!' 'No – I'd charge the same price with or without za'atar,' the chef counters. 'The za'atar is a free gift from my soul.'

Eyal Shani wipes a large stone clean. 'You have no idea what you're about to experience: I'm going to give you all the smells, colours and flavours of Israeli cuisine on one plate.' The most celebrated chef in the country is about to prepare breakfast for me in his self-styled back garden. A little later we're mopping the last remnants of an improvised salad of labneh and wild za'atar from the warm limestone, using torn pieces of bread. It's the most heavenly breakfast I've ever eaten. And the most illegal. Eyal Shani laughs: 'That's what makes it taste so good.'

Recipe on page 259.

LABNEH WITH ZA'ATAR, TOMATOES AND ONION

Serves 2–4

500 g (1 lb 2 oz/2 cups) full-fat goat's-
    milk yoghurt (3.5% fat or above)
500 g (1 lb 2 oz/2 cups) Turkish yoghurt
    (10% fat or above)
1 teaspoon salt
12 oregano sprigs
6 thyme sprigs
2 large ripe vine tomatoes, cut in half
1 medium onion, finely chopped
1 mild Turkish green capsicum (pepper),
    finely chopped
extra virgin olive oil
2–4 pittas or laffa (page 300)

In the absence of fresh za'atar (see page 256), we'll have to rough it with oregano and thyme. Try to source the best you can find: avoid at all times, but especially for this recipe, tasteless supermarket oregano. Good-quality oregano can be identified by its small, velvety leaves – bite one between your front teeth and it should make your tongue tingle. If you have a Middle Eastern corner shop in your neighbourhood, that's where you'll have a good chance of finding not only quality oregano but also the long, pale-green Turkish capsicums that I use in this recipe, which look and taste like a cross between pointed capsicums and chillies. If you can't get hold of this type of capsicum, use a deseeded, thinly sliced green chilli.

To make the labneh, line a bowl with a piece of muslin (cheesecloth), add both types of yoghurt and mix in the salt. Bring the edges of the muslin together and tie tightly with cooking string to form a pouch. Hang this pouch in the refrigerator somehow (I tie it to the metal drinks rack), still suspended over the bowl to catch the strained liquid. (If you can't make this work, then place the pouch into a fine-mesh sieve and suspend that over the bowl – this takes more time, but it should be ready after 24 hours in the refrigerator.)

Meanwhile, preheat the oven to 50°C (120°F). Lay the sprigs of oregano and thyme on a roasting tray and place in the centre of the oven for 3 hours, to dry out.

When ready to serve, spread about half of the labneh onto a large sharing plate using the bottom of a spoon (the remaining labneh can be kept in the refrigerator for a few days, for use in another recipe – see page 255). Squeeze the tomato halves over the labneh to release the seeds and juice. Sprinkle over the onion and capsicum. Strip the leaves from the dried oregano and thyme sprigs and sprinkle over the labneh. Drizzle with olive oil and serve with the bread.

130 g (4½ oz) pine nuts

160 g (5¾ oz/1⅔ cups) pecans, unsalted

100 g (3½ oz/⅔ cup) sesame seeds

2 red chillies, sliced into thin rings

250 g (9 oz/3⅓ cups) white cabbage, shredded

3 spring onions (scallions), sliced into rings

125 g (4½ oz) bean sprouts

50 ml (1¾ fl oz) white vinegar

75 ml (2½ fl oz) extra virgin olive oil

35 g (1¼ oz) caster (superfine) sugar

35 ml (1¼ fl oz) soy sauce (preferably a low-salt version)

EASTERN-STYLE NUT SALAD

Jews emigrated to Israel from all corners of the world – apart from (with a few exceptions) Asia. Nevertheless, modern-Israeli fusion cuisine is steeped in Asian influences. For example, after Tokyo and New York, Tel Aviv has the highest number of sushi restaurants per inhabitant. A fondness for Asian cuisine can be traced back to the holiday time that tens of thousands of Israelis put in each year in Asian countries stretching from India to Japan. Straight after their military service (three years of daily stress and iron discipline for boys; two years for girls), most young people grab their rucksack and head east to blow off some steam. India and Nepal are especially popular destinations due to their readily available drugs, hippy-trippy reputation, vast expanses of nature, low prices and well-loved cuisine. As well as a shocking number of psychoses and drug addictions, after a riotous year out, these former soldiers also return home with a passion for Asian cuisine – and you can see this reflected in Tel Aviv's restaurants.

Toast first the pine nuts, then the pecans, then the sesame seeds in a dry frying pan until pale golden brown – shake the pan regularly to prevent the nuts and seeds from burning (although if the pecans get a little scorched that's not a problem). Take care when toasting the sesame seeds, because they pop in all directions. Set the nuts and seeds aside to cool and transfer to an airtight container until ready to serve.

Mix the chillies, cabbage, spring onions and bean sprouts in a bowl. Whisk the vinegar, oil, sugar and soy sauce in a separate bowl until combined.

Just before serving, pour the dressing over the salad and toss to combine. Add the toasted nuts and seeds and toss again.

This salad can be kept in the refrigerator for 1 day.

BLACK QUINOA WITH ROASTED CAPSICUMS, RADISHES AND BLACK OLIVES

Serves 4–8

125 g (4½ oz) black quinoa
2 yellow capsicums (bell peppers)
125 g (4½ oz/1 cup) radishes, trimmed
  and sliced
80 g (2¾ oz/½ cup) pitted kalamata olives,
  sliced
125 g (4½ oz) feta, crumbled
75 g (2¾ oz/½ cup) salted cashew nut
  halves
75 ml (2½ fl oz) extra virgin olive oil
2 tablespoons red wine vinegar
1 tablespoon maple syrup
salt and freshly ground black pepper
15 g (½ oz/¾ cup) mint leaves, roughly
  chopped

I can still remember the first time I ate quinoa. It was a decade ago in Orna and Ella, a charming café on Sheinkin Street, which recently closed its doors after 25 years. Orna, or Ella (I never did find out who was who, which is often the curse of famous duos – which one is Laurel and which one is Hardy?) came over to my table to explain to me that the shiny balls in my salad weren't grains, but the medicinal super-seeds of the ancient Incas. Since then, quinoa has conquered the world – in no small part thanks to the evangelism of the Israeli cookbook author Yotam Ottolenghi. That the Israelis discovered quinoa 'early' (I'm using quotation marks because this timing is relative, quinoa having been grown for thousands of years before the Israelis started cooking with it) is not surprising: the South American seed seems to have been made with salad-loving Israelis in mind. Quinoa makes an excellent (gluten-free) alternative to bulgur (bulgur wheat) in tabouleh or a tasty addition to the classic Israeli salad (page 252). I like red or black quinoa best – they're crispier, with a more peppery flavour than white quinoa.

According to the packet instructions, quinoa should be prepared like rice: that is, one part quinoa is cooked in two parts water. However, Orna and Ella swore by the pasta method: they boiled their quinoa in plenty of salted water until al dente. I've tried both methods and the difference in taste and texture is negligible, but I'd recommend the pasta method for convenience.

Pour the quinoa into a fine-mesh sieve and rinse under cold running water. Bring a large saucepan of salted water to the boil, add the rinsed quinoa, reduce the heat to low and cook for 12–15 minutes, until al dente. Drain and set aside to cool.

Meanwhile, blacken the capsicums over the open flame of your hob, or, if you don't have a gas cooker, under the grill (broiler) (see instructions on page 298). Seal in zip-lock bags and set aside to cool. Once cooled, remove the skins, stalks and seeds and slice the flesh into thin strips.

Mix the quinoa, roasted capsicums, radishes, olives, feta and nuts together in a large serving bowl. In a separate bowl, whisk the olive oil, vinegar and maple syrup until combined, then season with freshly ground black pepper. Just before serving, pour the dressing over the salad, sprinkle over the mint and mix well. Taste and season with salt, if desired.

Serves 4–8

125 g (4½ oz) red quinoa
8 oregano sprigs, leaves only
1 red chilli
200 g (7 oz) smoked turkey, shredded
80 g (2¾ oz/½ cup) pitted kalamata olives,
    halved
100 g (3½ oz/½ cup) marinated artichoke
    hearts, finely chopped
100 g (3½ oz/⅔ cup) semi-dried (sun-
    blushed) cherry tomatoes
2 teaspoons za'atar
90 ml (3 fl oz) extra virgin olive oil
2 tablespoons red wine vinegar
salt and freshly ground black pepper

RED QUINOA
WITH SMOKED TURKEY

Trade the red quinoa for black and the turkey for chicken if
you prefer, but I strongly recommend that you don't substitute
the semi-dried tomatoes, which have a much softer texture
and more subtle flavour than sun-dried tomatoes. The best are
semi-dried cherry tomatoes, but the majority of supermarkets
and delicatessens don't stock these. If you do find them, buy a
lot: if stored well, they keep for years.

Pour the quinoa into a fine-mesh sieve and rinse under cold running
water. Bring a large saucepan of salted water to the boil, add the rinsed
quinoa, reduce the heat to low and cook for 12–15 minutes, until al
dente. Drain and set aside to cool.

Strip the leaves from the oregano sprigs. Remove the stalk from the
chilli and rub the chilli back and forth between your palms, shaking out
the seeds as you go; slice the chilli into rings. Add the quinoa, turkey,
olives, artichoke hearts, oregano, chilli, cherry tomatoes and za'atar
to a large serving bowl and mix well.

In a separate bowl, whisk the olive oil and vinegar until well combined
and season with freshly ground black pepper. Dress the salad gradually
with this mixture (you may not need all of the dressing). Before serving,
taste and season with salt if necessary.

See photo on page 262.

RED TABOULEH

Serves 4

2 large, deep-red beetroots (beets), peeled
    and cut into cubes
125 g (4½ oz/¾ cup) medium-grain
    bulgur (burghul)
1 red chilli
large bunch of flat-leaf (Italian) parsley
½ bunch of mint
2 spring onions (scallions), trimmed and
    sliced into rings
100 g (3½ oz/⅔ cup) feta, crumbled
50 g (1¾ oz/½ cup) walnuts, broken into
    pieces
juice of 1 lemon
extra virgin olive oil
salt and freshly ground black pepper

When it comes to *salatim*, tabouleh (pronounced with emphasis on the 'ou') cannot be left out. This salad, in its various guises, is hugely popular throughout the region, and in Israel, at least half of the dish consists of chopped fresh parsley. Fresh mint is also almost always added, plus a modest amount of bulgur (bulgur wheat). Outside the Levant, raw couscous is often used as a substitute, but I advise you to try the recipe with bulgur – just soak it in cold water for half an hour before you start. If you replace the tap water with beetroot water, as in this recipe, the bulgur will turn a beautiful purple-red colour and become imbued with a subtly sweet flavour that screams out for a salty foil such as feta. Make sure you ask your greengrocer for beetroot that are a deep-red colour inside, not yellow or marbled, because otherwise the bulgur will be coloured orangey-brown at best.

Put the beetroot and 400 ml (14 fl oz) of water into a large saucepan and bring to the boil. Reduce the heat until the water is simmering and continue to cook for 20 minutes. Drain the beetroot through a fine-mesh sieve suspended over a bowl and collect the cooking water in the bowl. Set this beetroot water aside to cool.

Once the beetroot water has cooled, soak the bulgur in the water for a good 30–40 minutes, until soft enough to eat but with a bit of bite left. Drain and set aside.

Meanwhile, remove the stalk from the chilli and roll the chilli back and forth between your palms, shaking out the seeds as you do so. Slice the chilli into rings. Slice the parsley and mint leaves carefully – don't chop them haphazardly, because then the herbs will release their precious oils and go mushy.

Just before serving, mix together the bulgur, diced beetroot, chilli, herbs, spring onions, feta and walnuts. Dress with the lemon juice and a good glug of olive oil, and season to taste with salt and freshly ground black pepper.

100 g (3½ oz) drained, tinned, MSC-
    certified tuna, in oil (approx 2 × 140 g/
    5 oz tins)
2 spring onions (scallions), sliced into
    thick rings
½ granny smith (or other tart green
    apple), peeled, cored and diced
8 pitted green olives, sliced
1 green chilli (to taste), deseeded and
    sliced into rings
1 teaspoon capers, drained
3 tablespoons mayonnaise
1 teaspoon dijon mustard
salt and freshly ground black pepper
4 pittas
handful of salted, crinkle-cut chips
    (crisps) to serve

PITTAS FILLED WITH TUNA, APPLE, CAPERS AND CRINKLE-CUT CHIPS

A bowl of tuna salad is a staple of the Israeli breakfast – it usually consists of little more than flakes of tinned tuna mixed with olive oil or mayonnaise, and seasoned with black pepper and salt. This might sound joyless, but it's precisely because of its simplicity that tuna salad goes so well with the contents of all those other dishes on the breakfast table: the Israeli salad, the tahini, the cottage cheese and the cream cheeses.

The rich tuna salad in this recipe is more suited to lunch, or to a hearty snack when hunger strikes. If your pantry is a bit like mine, you might find you already have all the ingredients, except for the chips. If that's the case, then I'm afraid you'll still need to pop to the shops, because crinkle-cut chips are the secret to the success of this dish. They give the creamy tuna filling a welcome salty crunch, and stop it from making the velvety pitta too soggy.

Add the tuna to a large bowl and mash with a fork. Stir in the spring onions, apple, olives, chilli (to taste), capers, mayonnaise and mustard. Season to taste with salt and freshly ground black pepper.

Toast the pittas until heated through but still soft. Slice open the pittas and fill them with alternate layers of tuna salad and chips.

WATERMELON SALAD WITH APPLE, GRAPEFRUIT AND FETA

Serves 4

100 g (3½ oz/¾ cup) blanched hazelnuts
½ small watermelon, skin removed, flesh cut into cubes or triangles
2 granny smiths (or other tart green apples), sliced into strips
80 g (2¾ oz/½ cup) pitted kalamata olives, drained
2 red grapefruits, peeled and segmented
juice of 1 lime
200 g (7 oz) feta, cubed
4 mint sprigs, leaves roughly chopped

Watermelon and feta are as integral to the beaches of Tel Aviv as strawberries and whipped cream are to Wimbledon. This comparison is less far-fetched than it might seem at first glance. The Israeli coast acts as a series of informal courts for games of *matkot*, a non-competitive sport similar to beach tennis, with a rubber ball and wooden rackets (the *matkot*). Although this game has no winners or losers, it is still taken very seriously. From the break of day to when the sun slides below the sea line, the puck-puck-puck of *matkot* balls being hit from player to player almost drowns out the sound of the waves. In between games, players refuel with limonana (page 85) and watermelon-and-feta salad.

The trio of watermelon, feta and mint is so perfect that you'll rarely come across watermelon salads made with anything else. But that doesn't mean we can't jazz it up a bit, without meddling with the basic holy trinity. Watermelon is also a fantastic match with grapefruit and tart apple – not only do the sweet-sour flavours complement each other well, the contrasting textures also add interest.

Toast the hazelnuts in a dry frying pan until golden brown, then transfer them to a bowl and set aside to cool. Once cooled, chop coarsely.

Carefully mix the watermelon, apple, olives and grapefruit segments in a serving bowl. Drizzle over the lime juice, then top with the feta and mint and garnish with the toasted hazelnuts.

ROAST CHICKEN SALAD

Serves 4

80 g (2¾ oz/½ cup) blanched almond
    halves
1 eggplant (aubergine)
salt and freshly ground black pepper
around 450 g (1 lb) cooked left-over roast
    chicken meat (see intro)
1 large ripe avocado, peeled, pitted and
    flesh diced
200 g (7 oz) seedless white grapes, cut in
    half lengthways
10 oregano sprigs, leaves chopped
juice of ½ lemon
½ teaspoon dijon mustard
60 ml (2 fl oz/¼ cup) extra virgin olive oil
1 teaspoon honey (optional)

Every true Jewish family occasionally finds itself faced wtih the sizeable leftovers of a considerably larger-than-needed roast chicken, bought over-optimistically for Shabbat (after all, you never know who will stop by); they have also developed the necessary recipes with which to dispatch it. This salad is my favourite way to bring a half-eaten chicken back to life. However, the belly wants what it wants, and if you find yourself in front of an empty fridge with an uncontrollable hankering for roast chicken salad, then just buy some chicken thighs from the butcher – the meat is juicier and tastier than chicken breast. The only drawback is that chicken thighs are somewhat smaller and more irregularly shaped, but that doesn't matter for a salad. Grill (broil) them for a few minutes to brown the skin, then wrap them in foil and roast in the oven for about ten minutes. Having said that, no one will judge you for roasting a whole chicken just to make this salad. If you do this, then remember to double all the other ingredients, and be prepared to eat chicken salad until it starts coming out of your ears, because there's no left-over recipe for left-over chicken salad.

Toast the almonds in a dry frying pan until golden brown. Transfer to a bowl and set aside to cool.

Blacken the eggplant over the open flame of your hob, or, if you don't have a gas stove, in the oven under the grill (broiler) (see instructions on page 299). Set the eggplant aside to cool slightly, then peel off the blackened skin. Sprinkle the flesh with salt and set aside to drain in a colander or fine-mesh sieve, or on paper towel. Once drained, chop into pieces.

Pick the chicken meat from the carcass and cut it into pieces. Add it to a large serving bowl with the almonds, eggplant, avocado, grapes and oregano leaves.

Whisk the lemon juice with the mustard in a bowl until well combined. Gradually pour in the oil in a thin stream, whisking continuously, until the dressing is thick and emulsified. Whisk in the honey, to taste, if desired.

Just before serving, toss the salad in the dressing and season to taste with salt and freshly ground black pepper.

VEGETARIAN CHOPPED LIVER

Serves 4

2 eggplants (aubergines)
splash of sunflower oil
5 onions, peeled
1 tablespoon brown sugar
pinch of salt
100 g (3½ oz/1 cup) walnuts
3 eggs, hard-boiled

Chopped liver, an unflattering name for coarse chicken-liver pâté, is one of the most famous of all Ashkenazi dishes. It's not a dish that you'll often find on the menu in Tel Aviv's restaurants, but in many households it's a fixture of the Friday-night dinner that heralds the start of Shabbat. Things were different halfway through the last century, in the early years of the Jewish state: meat and poultry were generally scarce and therefore unaffordable, so this alternative, made with eggplants instead of chicken livers, became very popular.

Today, chicken is no longer scarce. In fact, according to statistics, Israel is the world's biggest consumer of poultry, with the average Israeli eating 58 kilos (128 pounds) every year. The Americans come second, putting away 49 kilos (108 pounds) per person, while my fellow Dutchies don't even manage half of that (we eat a paltry 22 kilos – 49 pounds – annually per head). The popularity of poultry in Israel is in large part due to the extremely low consumption of pork. Israel also has an extensive poultry industry, which was established in the sixties with the help of government subsidies.

Despite the Israelis' love of chicken, the vegetarian version has never fallen completely out of favour. In fact, this ersatz throwback recently enjoyed a revival in restaurants. It fits well with the fashionable nostalgia for the good old days – which in reality were not nearly as good as our rose-tinted memories would have us believe. Nostalgic or not, this is one tasty dish.

Blacken the eggplants over the open flame of your hob, or, if you don't have a gas stove, under the grill (broiler) (see instructions on page 299). Set the eggplants aside to cool slightly, then peel off the blackened skin.

Cover the base of a frying pan with a thin layer of sunflower oil and set over low heat. Grate the onions into the pan, stir in the sugar and a good pinch of salt, and fry for 15 minutes, until softened and translucent, stirring regularly to prevent them from sticking.

Meanwhile, grind the walnuts into rough crumbs using a mortar and pestle. After the onions have been cooking for 15 minutes, stir in the walnuts and continue to fry for 15–20 minutes, until the onions are dark brown and pleasantly sweet. Remove from the pan and set aside to cool.

Mince all of the ingredients using a meat grinder positioned to its finest setting, or blitz with a hand-held blender until just combined. Season to taste with salt and freshly ground black pepper. Serve with freshly baked challah bread (page 297) and tahini.

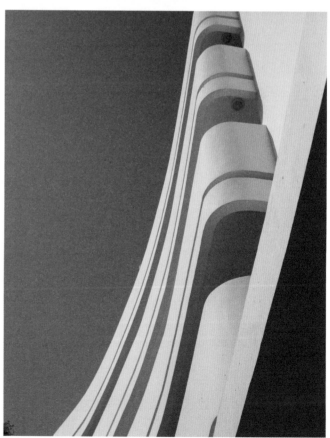

BASIC RECIPES

100 g (3½ oz) raw tahini
1–2 tablespoons lemon juice
1 roasted garlic clove (optional)
   (page 286)
pinch of salt

Using a hand-held blender, mix the raw
tahini with the lemon juice and garlic
(if using). It will start to stiffen. Keep
blending and gradually add a few drops
of water at a time, until the sauce has
the consistency of a salad dressing.
Season to taste with salt.

Like almost everyone, I always used to
add garlic to my tahini, but nowadays
I usually leave it out. During my time
in the restaurant kitchens of Tel Aviv I
learned that the acidic flavours of the
tahini come to the fore in the absence of
garlic. Sometimes garlic genuinely adds
something to the sauce, for example
when it's being served with roasted
eggplant (aubergine). In such cases I
like to add roasted garlic (page 286),
because the resulting tahini is milder
and smoother. You can be far more
generous with roasted garlic than with
raw garlic – keep tasting the sauce as
you add the garlic.

TAHINI

It's virtually impossible to overstate the importance of tahini
in modern Israeli cuisine. The sesame-seed paste is popular
throughout the region, but nowhere is it as omnipresent as
in Israel. Tahini is an indispensable ingredient in our three
favourite pitta sandwiches (falafel, shawarma and sabich), but
it's so much more than just a snack-bar sauce. Even the best
restaurants in Tel Aviv get through litres of the stuff every day.
Basically, if you don't like tahini, then you'll have a hard time in
Israel. I can think of only one other world cuisine with a similar
obsession with a single sauce: what soy sauce means to the
Japanese is what tahini means to the Israelis.

Personally, I think tahini is the most wonderful sauce in the
world. It's quick and easy to make and takes every dish to the
next level. Although its lush, creamy texture might suggest
otherwise, tahini contains substantially fewer calories than
notorious fat smugglers such as mayonnaise, hollandaise,
béchamel and garlic sauce. Moreover, unlike many other sauces,
it's vegan and therefore *parve* (see page 313), which means that
orthodox Jews can slather it over meat, fish and dairy to their
heart's content.

My favourite brands of tahini are Al Arz from Nazareth and
Har Bracha, Karawan and Al-Jamal from Nablus. This town,
located in the northern part of the West Bank, is considered
the tahini capital of the Middle East. In stark contrast to the
BDS activists, who are trying to serve the Palestinian cause by
boycotting Israeli products, Palestinian tahini manufacturers
are targeting the Israeli market. Rabbis act as supervisors in
their factories, so that the tahini can be officially declared
kosher. The plastic tubs that make their way to Tel Aviv in
trucks strikingly often have logos upon which peace doves are
prominently displayed.

Tahini section in an Eden Teva supermarket

ROASTED GARLIC

8–10 bulbs of solo or pearl garlic (see
   introduction) or 1 large bulb
   of normal garlic
splash of extra virgin olive oil

Okay, so the metamorphosis of raw garlic to roasted garlic is not
quite in the same league as that of caterpillar to butterfly, corn
to popcorn, Joy Division to New Order, Bruce Banner to Hulk
or, indeed, Sharon Cohen to Dana International. However, after
an hour in the oven, the flavour of those garlic cloves is pretty
unrecognisable. Gone is the sharp, heartburn-inducing, in-your-
face garlic pong, and in its place is a pleasantly sweet flavour
and slightly smoky aroma. Another advantage to roasted garlic
is that it emerges from the oven as a butter-soft purée, so you
can just stir it into your sauce rather than endlessly chopping or
crushing it to work out the lumps. And who knows, your breath
might even stink a bit less than with raw garlic.

For inexplicable reasons, normal garlic bulbs from the
supermarket are always half the size of the ones at the
greengrocer. However, larger supermarkets also sell onion-sized
bulbs (known as solo or pearl garlic), which consist of just one
giant clove. Sourcing solo garlic will save you a lot of fiddling
with skins if you're preparing a particularly garlicky dish; also,
thanks to its somewhat milder taste, solo garlic is perfectly
suited to roasting.

Preheat the oven to 190°C (375°F).

Slice the bottom off each wet garlic bulb and drizzle the cut sides with
olive oil. Wrap each bulb in aluminium foil then transfer them to a
roasting tin and roast in the oven for 45 minutes. The garlic cloves are
ready when they have a glossy, slightly translucent appearance without
being browned, and slide easily from their skins.

If you can't find wet garlic, source the largest garlic bulbs you can, slice
off the tops and proceed as above, roasting for only 35–40 minutes.

The roasted garlic cloves can be stored in airtight jars, wrapped in their
aluminium foil. If stored in the refrigerator they will keep for at least a
week and a half.

CARAMELISED ONIONS

2 kg (4 lb 6 oz) large onions
splash of olive oil
1 tablespoon salt
1 tablespoon balsamic vinegar

Caramelising onions is a time-consuming but simple job that gives indescribably good results. I usually dedicate a Sunday afternoon to the task, because I can do it while the football's on. My team, Ajax, usually plays so pathetically that I can get up every so often to stir the pan without missing anything. Make a large batch that will keep you going for weeks.

Before you start, make sure you don't need to go anywhere for at least two hours. Peel and roughly chop the onions.

Heat a little olive oil in a 6 litre (200 fl oz) saucepan on the largest ring of your hob. Add the onions and fry them over high heat, stirring constantly, until translucent. Do not let them brown.

Reduce the heat and add the salt. Constant stirring is now no longer necessary – just move the onions about every few minutes, scraping any that have stuck to the bottom of the pan with a wooden spatula (add a splash of water to the pan, if necessary, to make this easier).

After about 1½ hours, when the onions have started to colour, add the balsamic vinegar and increase the heat slightly. Keep stirring regularly for another 30 minutes or so, until the onions are deep brown in colour and stick together as you stir them. Transfer the onions to a sterilised, airtight jar – they will keep for weeks in the refrigerator.

2 tablespoons ground cumin

1 tablespoon ground coriander

2 teaspoons ground cloves

1 teaspoon ground ginger (from the dried root)

2 teaspoons ground turmeric (from the dried root)

1 tablespoon ground cinnamon (from about 1 stick)

2 teaspoons ground allspice

½ teaspoon ground chilli or cayenne pepper

½ teaspoon ground cardamom seeds (from about 6 pods)

1 teaspoon ground nutmeg

2 teaspoons smoked paprika

TLV SPICE MIX

The Middle East has created various spice blends, all of which, for me, are just as nice as each other. Ras el hanout and baharat are the most well known. Both are readily available, although their generic names mask how diverse each different blend can actually be. Baharat just means 'spices' in Arabic, and ras el hanout loosely translates as 'the best of the store' – so the spices that end up in each blend depend on both the personal preferences of the grocer and the quality of his goods. The same applies to *hawaij*, a Yemeni blend of herbs and spices popular in Israel. *Hawaij* is traditionally used to flavour either soup or Yemeni coffee, depending on its composition. But the soup blend is also excellent in tagines, meat dishes and barbecue marinades.

My own TLV spice mix is a cross between these three blends. To make it, every once in a while I get out my spice mill – an old-fashioned looking device that's sold as a poppy-seed mill in good cookery shops and that grinds whole spices into powder in no time. Invest in one, and for the price of a bottle of wine (a good one, mind) you'll have a machine that will give you a lifetime of pleasure. Of course, you could just mix ready-ground spices and store them in a jam jar. But then you'd miss out on the aroma of the freshly ground spices. Fifteen minutes of grinding spices is also a better stress-buster than yoga, acupuncture and electro-shock therapy combined. Still not convinced of the usefulness of a spice mill? Then turn back to page 109 – that delicious dessert can only be made with a spice mill. Chop chop – to the cook shop!

Note that the quantities above are for the ground spices, so if you're using a spice mill to grind them, you'll need larger quantities of the whole spices. Double-check each spice as you add it to the mix, as some quantities in the list are in teaspoons and others in tablespoons. Add the whole spices to your spice mill little by little, otherwise it will get clogged up and you'll need to keep unscrewing it and shaking out the stuck spices.

Position the grinders of the spice mill to their finest setting. Finely grind first the cumin seeds, then the coriander seeds, then the cloves, measuring the correct quantity of each ground spice into a sterilised, airtight jar. Using a mortar and pestle, crush first the ginger root, then the turmeric root, then the cinnamon stick,

then the allspice and lastly the dried chillies. Grind each crushed spice separately in the mill, measuring the correct quantity of each into the jar. Bruise the cardamom pods, pop out the black-brown seeds and feed these through the mill (discard the pods). Add the correct quantity to the jar.

The spice mill can now go back into the cupboard. You will need to finely grate the nutmeg (take care of your knuckles!), adding the correct quantity to the jar. Add the smoked paprika, too. (I actually grind dried peppers into my spice blend at home, but these are almost impossible to find outside of Israel, so use the most fragrant ground paprika that you can find.) Stir the spice mix, seal the jar and keep until needed.

QUICK ISRAELI SALAD

3 ripe tomatoes
2 Lebanese (short) cucumbers
1 spring onion (scallion)
4 flat-leaf (Italian) parsley sprigs
1 tablespoon lemon juice
splash of extra virgin olive oil
salt and freshly ground black pepper

This is the basic version of the salad that's served as a side dish in restaurants at breakfast. Yes, its name will raise a few eyebrows, since Arabs have been making the very same salad for centuries, but it is still Israeli through and through – not because it was invented there, but simply because Israelis can't live without it. Its popularity is due in part to the Jewish state's agricultural foundations: in the kibbutzes, after an early start in the fields, the community sat down to a breakfast made with the morning's harvest. The Israeli climate also plays a role, for a fresh vegetable salad is the best weapon with which to combat the stifling heat. 'We're the only country where every meal, including breakfast, is served with salad,' cookbook author Janna Gur told me when I asked her once to sum up Israeli cuisine. This simple version of the salad is a key element of pitta-based snacks such as falafel, sabich and shawarma.

Finely dice the tomatoes and cucumbers. Slice both the white and green parts of the spring onion into rings. Finely chop the leaves and stalks of the parsley. Mix everything together and season to taste with the lemon juice, olive oil, and salt and freshly ground black pepper.

4 pittas
splash of extra virgin olive oil
35 g (1¼ oz/⅓ cup) za'atar

PITTA CHIPS

In no time at all, you can transform your stale pittas into irresistibly crunchy crackers. You can either do this in the oven or on a chargrill pan – I recommend the latter as it's much quicker and the pitta chips get charred with nice stripes. No stale pittas to hand? This works just as well with fresh ones.

Toast the pittas briefly until each side comes loose and the pittas can be easily cut in half around their length.

WITH A CHARGRILL PAN
Heat a cast-iron chargrill pan over high heat. Rub the rough, bready side of each pitta half with olive oil and sprinkle with a little za'atar. Chargrill the pittas, oiled-side down, for 1 minute, or until dark-brown stripes appear on the underside. Cut into triangles and set aside to cool and crisp up.

IN THE OVEN
Preheat the oven to its hottest setting and switch on the grill (broiler). Add a baking tray (or a pizza stone, if you have one) to the oven, just under the grill, to heat up. Place the pitta halves, rough-sides facing downwards, onto the tray or stone and grill until golden brown. Don't go anywhere, as this will happen quickly. Remove the pittas from the oven and brush the rough, bready side of each with the olive oil. Sprinkle with za'atar. Set aside to cool, then cut into triangles.

CHALLAH

Makes 2 loaves

30 g (1 oz) sugar
30 g (1 oz) fresh yeast (or 10 g/¼ oz
   dried yeast)
1 kg (2 lb 3 oz/6⅔ cups) strong flour
   (preferably type T65)
4 eggs
100 ml (3½ fl oz) sunflower oil
2 tablespoons salt
sesame or poppy seeds to decorate

Nothing beats the intoxicating smell of freshly baked challah that hangs over Tel Aviv on Friday mornings. In Lehamim, a bakery that's open day and night, you'll find challah piled high on mobile bread racks. They fill the shop floor in long parallel rows, so that, as a customer, you feel like you're wandering in a maze made from loaves instead of hedges. Behind the scenes, a small army of bakers work their socks off trying to keep pace with demand. When I'm in TLV, this is where I go on a Friday morning. Good challah might be two a penny in this city, but I wouldn't miss the challah theatre of Lehamim for anything.

Orthodox Jews bless the Sabbath with two challah loaves, but even for non-practising Israelis, no weekend is complete without this plaited (braided) bread. Even in Halutzim 3, one of the city's least kosher restaurants (now sadly closed), challah would sit on the table on Friday evenings. Filled with pork mince and bacon, but still.

Different challah loaves vary in taste, from dry and savoury to creamy and sweet. They're plaited using up to ten strands. Lehamim sells them elongated, circular or as wreath with an in-built glass tray for tahini or honey. Most of their challah tastes slightly sweet and has a cake-like texture thanks to the addition of eggs. At first glance, challah looks a bit like brioche, but the loaves are not made with butter, to accommodate orthodox customers – who, in observance of the Jewish law prohibiting the mixing of meat and dairy, would otherwise not
be able to fill their challah sandwiches with meat.

Dissolve the sugar in 250 ml (8½ fl oz/1 cup) of warm water. When the water has cooled to body temperature, stir in the yeast. Add a pinch of the flour and set the mixture aside for 15 minutes, by which time its surface should be foaming.

Shake the flour into a large mixing bowl (or the bowl of your free-standing mixer) and crack in 3 of the eggs. Add the oil and the yeast mixture, then knead, either using your hands or your electric mixer fitted with dough hooks. Continue to knead the dough for about 10 minutes, or until its texture is elastic – if the dough feels too tight, gradually add up to 300 ml (10½ fl oz) of lukewarm water during the kneading process, as needed. When you're happy with the dough, knead in the salt, then roll it into a ball, return it to the bowl, cover with a tea towel and leave in a warm room for at least 1 hour, to prove.

When the dough has proved, cut it in half. Make 3 long sausage shapes from one half of the dough, each about 3 cm (1¼ in) thick. Squash the ends of these lengths of dough together at one end, then plait them as you would your daughter's hair, by folding first the right length over the middle length, and then the left length over what has become the middle length. Squash the ends of the dough plait together at the other end. Fold both squashed ends under the loaf. Repeat the process with the remaining dough to make 2 loaves. If in doubt, hit up YouTube for instructional videos. Set the plaited challah loaves aside, uncovered, for another hour, then preheat the oven to 190°C (375°F) and line a baking tray with baking paper.

Beat the remaining egg in a bowl. Brush the loaves with the beaten egg and sprinkle generously with the sesame or poppy seeds. Bake in the middle of the oven for 20–25 minutes, until the bottom of the loaves make a hollow sound when tapped. If the tops get too dark too quickly, move the loaves to a lower shelf and reduce the oven temperature slightly.

ROASTED CAPSICUMS

Israeli chefs are more than happy to blacken their vegetables: the sugars within caramelise and add an extra dimension of sweetness to their already sweet native produce. If there's one fruit that's noticeably improved after a little flame-grilling, it's the capsicum (bell pepper). As a crudité, it's the low point of many a party spread; as part of an Israeli salad it's just about tolerable; as soon as it's roasted, it's a delicacy that can't be bettered. This goes for all colours of capsicum – except for green. All the fire in the world can't make those bad boys palatable.

OVER THE FLAMES OF YOUR GAS HOB
Balance red, yellow or orange capsciums on the pan supports of your biggest gas ring – you should be able to fit three on at a time. Turn on the heat and roast the capsicums, turning them regularly using kitchen tongs, until the skin is completely blackened all over.

IN THE OVEN
Preheat the oven to its hottest setting and switch on the grill (broiler). Cook the capsicums on a baking tray placed just under the grill, turning regularly, until the skin turns completely brown with occasional black spots on all sides.

Transfer the hot capsicums to zip-lock bags, seal and set aside to cool. Once cooled, scrape the charred skin from the fruit using a teaspoon or your fingers. Rinse off the last flakes under cold running water. Remove the stalk and seeds from the capsicums and gently pat the flesh dry with paper towel.

ROASTED
EGGPLANT

Of the many possible ways to cook eggplants (aubergines), *al ha'esh* ('over the flames') is by far the most popular. The flesh takes on an intensely smoky aroma, one that few people can immediately appreciate at first. But do yourself a favour and don't give up on it too soon, because it will end up being one of your favourite flavours. The best way to roast eggplants is to take *al ha'esh* literally and blacken them over the flames of your gas hob – or, even better, right on some glowing barbecue coals. If you don't cook on gas, you can achieve more or less the same result in the oven, although it requires a little more patience.

Buy eggplants that feel firm to the touch. Their colour doesn't affect their flavour, but the pale or marbled varieties have the advantage that you can clearly see which spots still need to be blackened.

ON THE GAS STOVE

If you're the owner of a squeaky-clean kitchen and want to keep it that way, then cover the metal plate surrounding the burner with foil. Balance two eggplants on the pan supports of your biggest gas ring. Turn on the heat and roast the eggplants for about 20 minutes in total, until the skin is completely blackened all over. Move the eggplants regularly using kitchen tongs, turning up the heat so that the flames reach the higher parts of the skin when necessary, and holding each eggplant upright over the flames using tongs in order to burn its base. Make sure no part of the skin escapes the flames.

IN THE OVEN

Preheat the oven to 250°C (480°F) and switch on the grill (broiler). Pierce the eggplants in several places using the tip of a sharp knife. Place the eggplants onto a grill shelf directly beneath the grill and slide a roasting tray underneath them on the next shelf down, to catch any drips. Roast for about 1 hour, turning every 15 minutes using tongs.

Remove the eggplants from the heat and set aside until cool enough to handle. Holding the eggplant by its stalk, scrape off the blackened skin, being careful to leave the flesh underneath as intact as possible. No matter how tempting it may be, never peel the eggplant under cold running water, because it will absorb the liquid like a sponge, and that unique smoky flavour you've been cultivating will be gone.

230 g (8 oz) plain (all-purpose) flour, plus
    extra for dusting
2 teaspoons caster (superfine) sugar
1 teaspoon salt
2–3 tablespoons extra virgin olive oil, plus
    extra for greasing
125 ml (4¼ fl oz/½ cup) water

In a large bowl, mix together the flour, sugar and salt. Mix in the olive oil using a fork. Gradually add the water in a thin stream, working it into the dry ingredients as much as possible using the fork. Turn the mixture out onto a lightly floured work surface and knead into a dough using your hands, repeatedly rolling it into a ball and stretching it away from you with your palm. Add extra water or flour if the dough is too dry or too wet. After 5 minutes, the dough should be elastic and just a little bit sticky. Roll it into a ball, rub it with a few drops of olive oil and return it to the bowl. Cover with plastic wrap and set aside to rest at room temperature for 30 minutes.

Cover the largest ring of your gas hob with the upside-down wok (see introduction) and heat until the sides are very hot. Carefully move the wok to a smaller gas burner and heat again until the top is very hot. If you don't have a suitably sized or shaped wok, or don't cook on gas, cook the laffa in a large frying pan (not turned upside down!). Note that this method of cooking will cause the flatbreads to shrink slightly, making them less thin.

Once the dough has rested, knead it well again and divide it into 4 evenly shaped balls. Dust your work surface lightly with flour, flatten one of the dough balls with your palm, then dust it with flour, too. Roll out the dough in one direction using a rolling pin. Give it a quarter-turn and roll out again. Repeat the process until the bread dough is round and wafer thin. Brush the surface lightly with olive oil.

LAFFA

Laffa is the Israeli version of a tortilla: a sort of large, savoury pancake that's eaten as a wrap, usually filled with shawarma, kebab meat or labneh. Laffa is also served alongside *salatim*. It's the ultimate finger food: you tear off a piece, fold it in half and use it as a spoon to scoop up your hummus and other dips.

Although this flatbread was introduced to Israel by Iraqi Jews (it's also known as Iraqi pitta), it's mainly sold by elderly Druze women. In an attempt to get my head around the art of making laffa, I regularly watched one such veiled granny at work at a stall halfway up the Carmel Market. During each visit to the market, I studied the acrobatic hand movements with which she deftly turned bits of dough into wafer-thin pancakes. Mobile phone in hand, I filmed how she used a round cushion to flip the circles of dough onto a *saj*, a red-hot convex hotplate that looks like a giant black kippah.

Let's just say that I'm not cut out to be either a juggler or a laffa baker. Fortunately, you can also make the flatbreads with a rolling pin, even though it looks less spectacular and takes ten times longer. In the absence of a *saj*, I bought a large, round-bottomed wok that I turned upside down over the flames of the gas hob; it worked really well. By searching for 'saj pillow', I also managed to buy an authentic Druze cushion off eBay, which meant that I could still serve my laffa at the table with some necessary theatre.

If you are fortunate enough to own a sturdy, round and heat-resistant pillow, stretch the dough over it and flip it in one fluid movement onto the upturned wok. Whether you use a pillow or not, the idea is to get the dough to cover the wok with as few wrinkles as possible.

Bubbles should form on the surface of the dough almost immediately (if this doesn't happen, the wok isn't hot enough). Brush the top of the laffa with olive oil and cook it for 45 seconds, then turn it over and cook for a further 15 seconds.

Remove the cooked laffa from the heat and set aside on a platter, covered with a clean plastic bag and a clean, dry tea towel (this stops them from becoming crunchy and breaking when you try to make a wrap from them).

Cook the remaining flatbreads in the same way, wiping the surface of the wok clean with paper towel after each has been cooked. Serve the laffa as soon as possible – they are at their best when freshly baked.

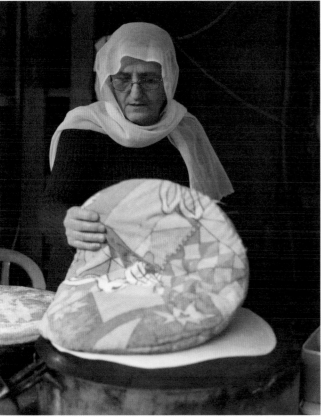

SEPHARDIC BROWN EGGS

Makes 10

10 eggs
at least 2 handfuls of onion skins (the
     more, the merrier)
1 tablespoon whole coffee beans
2 bags of black tea (about 2 teaspoons)
1 tablespoon olive oil
1 teaspoon salt

Everybody knows that you can hard-boil an egg in under
10 minutes – but you can also cook them for much longer. If you
cook them on a bed of onion peelings, you'll end up with eggs
whose whites are decorated with beautiful chestnut-brown
marbling and whose yolks are particularly velvety. These
magical brown eggs were introduced to Israel by the Yemeni
Jews. Because cooking on Shabbat is forbidden, they would
prepare a meat stew called *chamin* on Friday afternoon, which
would simmer away in the oven or on a hot plate. As well as
containing meat, rice and vegetables, the dish also included eggs,
which were eaten separately for breakfast on Saturday morning.
This is hardly done any more – these days, Sephardic brown
eggs are usually cooked separately with sabich (page 40) in mind,
or served as a topping for hummus.

At home, we never throw away our onion and garlic peels; instead we store them in a zip-lock bag in the vegetable drawer of our refrigerator. If you ask your greengrocer nicely, they might give you some loose onion skins. If your greengrocer is mean, or if you're too embarrassed to ask, just peel six large onions and keep the peeled onions in the fridge in a tightly sealed zip-lock bag until needed.

Bring a large saucepan of water to the boil. Add all of the ingredients to the water and return it to the boil, then reduce the heat until the water is simmering gently. Keep checking that the eggs are still covered with a layer of water – if the pan boils dry, the eggs can explode (and believe me, they like to wait until you peer into the pan to check the water level to do so ...). After about 3 hours, use the tip of a sharp knife to very carefully crack the egg shells. Continue to cook the eggs for half an hour, by which time the egg whites should be covered in a pretty, marbled pattern.

3 red capsicums (bell peppers)

2 kg (4 lb 6 oz) vine tomatoes

olive oil for frying

6 large garlic cloves, roughly chopped

1 red chilli, sliced

1 teaspoon paprika

1 teaspoon ground cumin

1–2 teaspoons sugar, plus extra to season

70 g (2½ oz) tomato paste
  (concentrated purée)

2 teaspoons salt

salt and freshly ground black pepper

MATBUKHA

As part of its range, just about every manufacturer of Israeli salads and dipping sauces makes – alongside the traditional top three of hummus, tahini and *salat chatzilim* (baba ghanoush) – a version of *matbukha*. This spicy sauce of tomatoes and roasted capsicums is North African in origin, but the recipe journeyed with the many Jewish Maghreb people who emigrated to Israel in the 1940s and 1950s. It's now one of the standard welcome snacks served at informal Sephardic restaurants.

No factory-produced sauces taste as good as the homemade versions, and this is especially true of matbukha. This recipe makes a large quantity of the sauce, since it's so easy to freeze and thaw in batches.

The nice thing about matbukha is that it's so full of flavour, it manages to take any dish with which it's served to another level. For example, you can serve it warm with Mediterranean-style meatballs, braise a fillet of cod in it, or use it to give a Middle Eastern twist to your pizza. Or just serve it as an appetiser with hummus, tahini and baba ghanoush, Tel Aviv style.

Blacken the capsicums over the flame of your hob, or, if you don't have a gas stove, under the grill (broiler) (see instructions on page 298). Seal them in zip-lock bags and set aside to cool. Then peel the skin from the capsicums – do this under water if necessary – and remove the stalks and seeds. Slice the flesh into strips.

Bring a saucepan of water to the boil. Score a cross shape into the bottom of each tomato using the tip of a sharp knife. Blanch one tomato at a time in the boiling water for 20–30 seconds. As you blanch the next tomato, refresh each just-blanched tomato under cold running water, then peel and set aside. Roughly chop the peeled tomatoes.

Heat a dash of olive oil in a heavy-based frying pan or cast-iron casserole pot. Add the garlic, chilli, paprika and cumin and fry for 1–2 minutes, stirring continuously until the garlic has softened. Add the tomatoes, capsicums, sugar, tomato paste and salt. Stir, then cover and reduce the heat to low. Simmer for 1 hour, then continue to cook, uncovered, for a further 1 hour, stirring occasionally, until really thick. Set aside to cool, then taste and season, if necessary, with salt, freshly ground black pepper and more sugar. Matbukha will keep in an airtight container in the refrigerator for at least 2 weeks; alternatively, freeze batches of it for later use.

RED CHRAIN

The preparation of this Ashkenazi sauce really is a piece of cake. The only challenge lies in finding fresh horseradish. In spring, most greengrocers stock a box of the roots, but once these have been sold, that's it. You can order it online: warehouses vacuum-pack horseradish so that it keeps forever.

Thanks to the recent revival of Ashkenazi cuisine in Israel (see page 139), chrain has regained some popularity in the Israeli kitchen. The sweet-sharp sauce is the classic accompaniment to well-known dishes such as tongue, gefilte fish and matzo-ball soup.

Makes 400 ml (13½ fl oz)

2 small cooked beetroot (beets)
200 g (7 oz) fresh horseradish root
90 ml (3 fl oz) red wine vinegar, plus extra to season
55 g (2 oz/¼ cup) sugar, plus extra to season
1 teaspoon salt

If you're not using ready-cooked, vacuum-packed beetroot, boil two unpeeled beetroot in a large saucepan of water. The problem is that the cooking time can vary dramatically: summer beetroot will be ready in half an hour, while winter beetroot can require up to 1½ hours. Just check in on them regularly during cooking: the beetroot are cooked through once you can pierce them easily with a fork. Drain and set aside until cool, then peel and roughly chop.

Meanwhile, open all the windows and doors in your kitchen, turn your extractor fan to its highest setting, and don your ski goggles. Peel the horseradish, cutting each root in half lengthways and discarding any hard, woody cores. Roughly chop the horseradish.

Purée all of the ingredients in a food processor until almost smooth. Taste and add extra sugar or vinegar if needed. Store in a sterilised, airtight jar in the refrigerator: the chrain will keep for at least 2 weeks.

2 cardamom pods, seeds only

1 teaspoon caraway seeds

2 teaspoons cumin seeds

3 jalapeños, deseeded (if desired) and
cut into large pieces

1 bunch coriander (cilantro), roughly
chopped

1 bunch flat-leaf (Italian) parsley, leaves
and stalks roughly chopped

3 garlic cloves

1 tablespoon lemon juice, plus extra
to season

extra virgin olive oil

pinch of salt

ZHUG

In Tel Aviv snack bars, customers all get asked the same question: *'rotze charief?'* ('do you want it hot?'). If you respond in the affirmative, the pitta-filler on duty will drizzle a spoonful of zhug over your falafel, shawarma or sabich. Depending on how the owner likes his zhug, this sauce will be anything from one thousand to one million on the Scoville scale. My advice is to never answer with a wholehearted yes, but to ask instead for *kzat* ('a little bit'). Unless, that is, you've always wanted to try fire-breathing.

Zhug can be green or red, depending on the type of chillies used. I prefer to use green jalapeños, which give my zhug the appearance of pesto. Make sure you warn people before they try it – especially any greedy children in your household (as my six-year-old daughter can attest).

Grind the cardamom seeds, caraway seeds and cumin seeds to a powder using a mortar and pestle.

Blitz the jalapeños, ground spices, herbs, garlic and lemon juice in a food processor until well combined. With the motor running, gradually add olive oil in a thin stream until the sauce resembles a thin pesto. Taste and season to taste with salt and, if necessary, a little extra lemon juice.

Store the zhug in an airtight container in the refrigerator. It will keep for at least 1½ weeks.

AMBA

Writing a cookbook is pure extravagance. The wastefulness begins as soon as you start developing a tasty idea into a tried-and-tested recipe: failures go straight in the bin, but what to do with five almost perfect versions of the same cake, all missing only the proverbial cherry? More wasteful still are the days when the photographer and food stylist come over for a photoshoot: at the end of the day I'm left with a dozen fantastic dishes to eat, and no guests. Fortunately on such occasions, I can always call my friend Shlomo.

Shlomo lives and works around the corner and has an insatiable appetite. What he can't manage to eat right then and there, he takes home with him. Shlomo once ate the chopped liver that I made for my cookery column in the *New Israelite Weekly* for four days straight – he remembers this as one of the high points of his bachelor life. Shlomo is also good for my self-confidence as a cook: he finds everything that I serve him equally legendary. Everything, that is, except my amba. This came as quite a shock to me, because Shlomo is proud of his Iraqi roots, and the spicy mango sauce was introduced to Israel by Iraqi immigrants. To reassure me, he told me that he didn't even like the version his very own grandmother, who hailed from Baghdad, used to make. In Israel he orders his sabich, against all unwritten laws, without amba. Fortunately, amba keeps for weeks in the refrigerator.

2 teaspoons fenugreek seeds
1 large unripe mango, peeled, pitted, flesh diced
175 g (6 oz) dried mango, very finely chopped
2 tablespoons honey
60 ml (2 fl oz/¼ cup) white wine vinegar
juice of 1 lemon
2 teaspoons coriander seeds
2 teaspoons cumin seeds
2 tablespoons sunflower or peanut oil
2 garlic cloves, finely chopped
1 tablespoon ground turmeric
2 teaspoons salt to season

Grind the fenugreek seeds to a powder using a mortar and pestle. Mix the fresh and dried mango, ground fenugreek, honey, vinegar and lemon juice in 400 ml (13½ fl oz) of water and bring to the boil. Reduce the heat until the mixture is simmering and simmer for 30 minutes, adding extra water if the mixture threatens to boil dry.

Meanwhile, grind the coriander and cumin seeds. Heat the oil in a frying pan over low heat and gently fry the garlic until softened but not coloured. Remove the pan from the heat and stir in the ground coriander and cumin to form a thick paste.

Transfer the mango mixture and the garlic mixture to the bowl of a food processor and add the turmeric. Blend to a smooth purée (this will take 5–10 minutes). Season to taste with the salt, adding a splash of water to loosen the sauce if necessary.

Makes 500 ml (17 fl oz) of schmaltz

2 kg (4 lb 6 oz) chicken skin, cut into
    pieces with a sharp knife
4 onions, roughly chopped
1 teaspoon salt

Due to the incomprehensible popularity of dry chicken-breast meat, slaughterhouses are left with mountains of chicken skin. This ends up as reclaimed meat for use in processed chicken dishes such as nuggets and meatballs. If you're lucky, your butcher might give you some chicken skins for free.

Heat two large, heavy-based saucepans over low heat and divide the chicken-skin pieces equally between them. Stir occasionally as you wait for the skins to release their fat. Be patient, and don't try to speed up the rendering process by increasing the heat.

After the chicken skin has been cooking for 30 minutes, divide the chopped onions and salt equally between the two pans and continue to cook for a further 20 minutes. Turn off the heat as soon as the onions and chicken-skin pieces are crisp and golden brown (these are your gribenes!).

Strain the contents of both pans through a fine-mesh sieve, collecting the strained liquid (the schmaltz) in a bowl or measuring cup. Transfer the schmaltz to a sterilised, airtight jar, seal and set aside to cool. Once cool, store in the refrigerator, where it will solidify (meaning that you can easily spoon what you need out of the jar). Stored in this way, schmaltz will keep for months.

Drain the gribenes on a plate lined with paper towel. Try your best to exert restraint as you snack on them.

SCHMALTZ AND GRIBENES

The most striking difference between Ashkenazi and Sephardic cuisine is the type of fat traditionally used to fry things. Before the global economy was established, there was an imaginary border separating northern and southern European and Asian countries. Vegetable oil was used in cooking anywhere south of this border, while countries north of the border depended on animal fats. Because kosher laws prohibit the mixing of dairy and meat products, Jews in the north relied on two types of fat: butter and schmaltz.

Schmaltz is the kosher alternative to lard. It's prepared in much the same way: the fat is rendered over low heat. The only difference is that schmaltz is made with chicken or goose skin, whereas lard is made from pork belly. The crispy remains are the kosher version of pork scratchings, called gribenes. Schmaltz became so synonymous with fatty Ashkenazi cuisine that even Ashkenazi biscuits (cookies) smelt faintly of chicken.

The era in which the pungent smell of schmaltz would emanate from the walls of Jewish homes is long gone: international trade has made all products available to everyone, and countries north of that imaginary border have since adopted healthier vegetable fats from the south. Also because plant based oils are suitable for both milk and meat dishes.

In Mediterranean Israel, olive oil and canola oil have always been widely available – upon arriving in the promised land in the late nineteenth century, Ashkenazi immigrants never had to make schmaltz again. Gefilte fish and latkes were still occasionally put on the table, but schmaltz found itself increasingly relegated due to a growing focus on healthy eating.

Thanks to the recent revival of Ashkenazi cuisine in Tel Aviv, schmaltz has also made a modest comeback. That's good news, because a spoonful of schmaltz makes everything tastier (try frying potatoes in it!). Another piece of good news is that those health warnings are not all that bad: butter actually contains more saturated fats than schmaltz. The real danger comes from the gribenes – they're fine if eaten in moderation, but that is easier said than done.

CHICKEN SOUP

Makes 5–6 litres (170–200 fl oz)

1 whole boiling chicken, cut in half, or
   2 kg (4 lb 6 oz) chicken carcasses
2 turkey necks (ask your butcher)
2 large onions, unpeeled, cut in half
5 garlic cloves, unpeeled
2 leeks, trimmed and sliced
2 carrots, sliced into rings
5 celery stalks (leaves intact), sliced
1 bunch of thyme
1 bunch of flat-leaf (Italian) parsley
2 bay leaves
10 peppercorns
salt to taste

Jewish folklore attributes health-giving powers to chicken soup, as long as it's homemade, preferably by an over-protective Yiddish *momme*. So much so that chicken soup is often called 'Jewish penicillin'. Apparently, this alleged medicinal effect has been demonstrated by serious scientists – although I think it's more of a Jewish placebo that only works if you believe in it yourself.

One of the big questions surrounding the making of chicken soup is how long to boil the chicken in the broth. There are those – among them Claudia Roden, the unrivalled chronicler of Jewish cuisine – who remove the chicken from the soup pot after just one hour. At this stage, the meat can still be used as the basis for another chicken dish, but the soup will need flavouring with stock (bouillon) powder. I understand that poor Ashkenazi households would traditionally want to get their money's worth from a pricey Shabbat chicken, but if you're not on a budget then you should leave the chicken boiling in the broth for as long as possible, so that it releases all of its flavour. You can choose whether to serve meat as part of the soup – personally, I prefer a clear broth, which can always be souped up (as it were) with meatballs, pitta croutons or matzo balls. I give the chicken meat to my dog, Strummer, over the course of a week. Chicken soup does not cost much to make nowadays, especially if you use chicken carcasses – butchers can't do anything with the carcasses so they'll probably give you one for free.

It's not surprising that chicken soup remains so well respected in Jewish cuisine – nothing beats the soothing smell of a large pan of chicken soup simmering on the stove. What's more, since it takes just as much time to make a large quantity as it does a small one, the best thing to do is to make and freeze a few litres, for use in risotto or to counter a sudden flu attack.

Fit the chicken halves (or carcasses) and the turkey necks as snugly as possible in the bottom of a whopper of a stockpot. Add the onions and garlic – their peel will give the broth its nice dark colour. Rinse the leeks, carrots and celery in a colander, then add them to the pan with the thyme, parsley, bay leaves and peppercorns, packing everything down tightly. Add 5 litres (170 fl oz) of water to the pan and bring to the boil, skimming the foam from the surface of the water regularly. Reduce the heat until the liquid is simmering and simmer for at least 3 hours on a low heat, skimming regularly.

Strain the broth through a colander into a second large saucepan. Season the strained broth with salt and set aside to cool. As the broth cools, the fat will float to the surface and solidify. You can remove this, but I recommend you leave it in the soup – it's precisely the chicken fat that gives the broth its delicious flavour.

ASHKENAZIM, ASHKENAZI
Literally: Germans, German. Used in Israel to refer to Jews from Christian countries (as opposed to Muslim countries). See also *Sephardim, Sephardic*.

BAGELS WITH LOX AND CREAM CHEESE
Well-known Jewish dish in America: a bagel spread with cream cheese and salmon.

BALADI
A word of Arabic origin indicating that a product is native and authentic.

BAR MITZVAH
Literally: son of the law. In Jewish law, a boy comes of age at thirteen; from then on he is responsible for his religious deeds. The usually lavish celebration party is about equal in size to the average wedding.

BAT MITZVAH
Literally: daughter of the law. Girls come of age a year earlier than boys, celebrating their bat mitzvah when they are twelve years old.

BDS MOVEMENT
Pro-Palestinian activist group that propagates the economic, cultural and academic boycott of Israel. BDS stands for 'Boycott, Divestment, Sanctions'.

BEN GURION
Israël's national airport, just outside Tel Aviv. Named after Israel's first prime minister, David Ben Gurion.

BETEAVON
'Enjoy your meal' (literally: 'on the appetite!').

CHAMETZ
See: Passover.

CHAREDIC
Literally: (god-)fearing. Name for ultra-orthodox Jews. Most of the *Charedim* in greater Tel Aviv live in the suburb of Bnei Brak, to the north-east of Tel Aviv.

CHOPPED LIVER
Coarse chicken-liver pâté with fried onions and hard-boiled eggs. A typical Friday-night Ashkenazi meal.

GEFILTE FISH
Ashkenazi classic: sweet braised fishballs, originally using carp or pike as a filling.

HUMMUSIA
Restaurant specialising in various hummus dishes served as main courses.

IVRIT
Modern Hebrew (in modern Hebrew).

JAFFA
Also known as Yafo or Joppa. Old Arabic port city that has been part of the municipality of Tel Aviv-Jaffa since 1950. The famous oranges of the same name aren't grown here – they were named after the port to which they were shipped. According to the Bible, Jaffa was the place where the prophet Jonah boarded a ship to flee his godly duties. Jaffa has 46,000 inhabitants, about 65 percent of whom are Jews and 35 percent Arabs.

KENYON
Covered shopping centre with indoor car park. The pinnacle of fun and entertainment in many Israeli cities. Despite the resemblance to a carved-out river valley, the word 'kenyon' has no relation to the American word 'canyon'. The name is a fusion of the Hebrew words for 'buy' and 'parking'. The *kenyon* is the perfect place to observe the average Israeli.

KIBBUTZ
Collective agricultural settlement where immigrants, mostly from Russia, settled from the beginning of the twentieth century. Their inhabitants were socialist, Zionist and generally non-religious. *Kibbutzniks* worked and ate together. Children lived together in a separate group. Private ownership was banned. Israel still has around 250 *kibbutzim* (plural for kibbutz), but collectivism has now virtually disappeared or is limited to a minimum.

KIBBUTZNIK
The inhabitant of a kibbutz.

LATKES
Ashkenazi potato pancakes. A traditional snack at Hanukkah.

L'CHAIM
Literally: 'to life'. A toast reserved for alcoholic drinks.

LERNEN
The study of religious texts in a *yeshiva*.

MSABBAHA
Coarse hummus, served warm.

NEBBISH
Yiddish: poor, unfortunate.

PARVE
Food and drink that contain neither dairy nor meat (including poultry): for example fruit, vegetables, grains, nuts, beans, eggs and fish. This is important because Jewish food laws forbid the mixing of meat and dairy products – beef cannot be fried in butter, and spaghetti bolognese can't be sprinkled with parmesan, for example. *Parve* literally means 'neutral', so these ingredients can be combined with either meat or dairy. After eating meat, practising Jews refrain from eating any dairy for either one, three or six hours, depending on their religious upbringing. Desserts that follow a meal that contains meat are therefore always *parve*.

PASSOVER
A seven-day celebration, held in March or April, that commemorates the Jews' exodus from Egypt. On the Seder, the first evening of Passover, stories about the Jews in slavery, the ten plagues and the exodus are recounted. According to the Passover story, because the Israelites had to flee quickly, they had no time to bake bread for the journey, and instead had to fill their knapsacks with crumbled matzo, the slave food that, after four centuries of oppression, they would rather have left behind. As a reminder of that little hitch in an otherwise well-oiled operation, matzo is the only grain product permitted during Passover. Other

grain products are called *chametz* and are strictly forbidden – not only to eat, but also to possess. As such, the cat must also convert to a grain-free diet during Passover. Judaism – which, some would argue, is not unextreme in its rules at the best of times – has no food law that must be more fundamentally observed than the ban on *chametz*. Weeks before Passover begins, observant Jews will turn the house upside down to find and flush out every last perfidious crumb – between the pages of a cookbook, for example, or in the sock drawer of a wardrobe. Kitchen utensils, crockery, cutlery, pots and pans are all replaced, and the kitchen counter covered with a custom-made protective layer. Products that even the worst-affected coeliacs can enjoy with no ill-effects are not automatically allowed at Passover. Your favourite brands of chocolate, soft drinks, dried herbs, butter, mayonnaise, toothpaste and cat food should be replaced with strictly controlled substitutes, which of course cost three times as much and are only half as tasty.

In Tel Aviv, most people buy some matzo to celebrate the Seder, and let the hassle of the other traditions pass them by.

SABRA
Prickly pear – a cactus fruit which, due to its spiky exterior and soft, sweet flesh, is used as a metaphor for native Israeli Jews. Also: an American-Israeli manufacturer of Mediterranean and Middle Eastern salads.

SCHMOOZE
To chat (Yiddish).

SEDER
The first evening of Passover. See also: Passover.

SEPHARDIM, SEPHARDIC
Literally: Spaniards, Spanish. Used in Israel to indicate Jews originally from Islamic countries (as opposed to Christian countries). See also *Ashkenazim, Ashkenazi*.

SHABBAT
The Jewish day of rest begins on Friday at twilight and ends on Saturday when the first stars appear in the sky. Thus, in December, Shabbat will already be underway in the afternoon, while in June it ends 'late at night'.

Whereas in ultra-religious Jerusalem, public life more or less grinds to a halt on Friday evening, in Tel Aviv the party is just getting started. However, Saturday is a quiet day in Tel Aviv, similar to our Sunday. In fact, Sunday is a normal working day – in Israel, the weekend starts a day earlier, on Friday. As such, the most popular nights for going out are Wednesday, Thursday and Friday.

Shabbat (*shabbos* in Yiddish) honours the day of rest that God observed after creating the world in six days. Religious Jews abstain from all activities on the Sabbath: they're forbidden not only from earning money and making purchases, but also from using fire or electricity. Cooking is therefore impossible, and smokers have to control their addiction for one day. Food for Shabbat is prepared before it starts and, where necessary, kept warm on special hot plates, since even turning on a switch is against the rules.

To that end, religious families use a timer to turn off the lights at bedtime.

As for mobile phones, they're put aside for the day, while the television remains off and the car sits on the drive. Above all else, nothing can be (de)constructed on Shabbat. This means that writing something down, sewing on a button, shaving, and cutting your nails are all prohibited. Even using toilet paper in the normal way infringes the rules, meaning that pious Jews need to tear up a few rolls before Shabbat.

Since music, sport, taking a shower, gardening, cycling, crafting, fishing and going out are also forbidden, most people spend their Shabbat eating, reading, praying, sleeping and making love.

Shavuot

Also known as the Feast of Weeks (*shavuot* literally means 'weeks'). So-named because Shavuot is celebrated in May or June, exactly seven weeks after Passover. Shavuot lasts just one day and commemorates the receiving by the Jewish people of the Ten Commandments and the Torah. Traditionally, a great deal of dairy products are eaten during Shavuot. This is to honour the day that the Jewish people received the Torah, with all its rules. Suddenly, everything they had been doing was no longer permissible, and for the first time, the rules around ritual slaughter were passed down. There was no other option but to throw away all the meat dishes that they had prepared for the festivities. To make matters worse, it was Shabbat, so no more animals could be slaughtered.

Fun fact: according to *gematria* (a kind of Jewish Scrabble), the Hebrew letters of the word *chalav* ('milk') are worth 40 points. This is exactly the number of days that Moses had to stay on Mount Sinai before he could receive the Torah.

Shekel

Israeli currency, symbolised with a ₪ and sub-divided into 100 *agurot*. In the early 1980s, the currency had to contend with a hyperinflation so huge that people joked that it was cheaper to travel by taxi in Israel than by bus – after all, you pay the bus fare at the beginning of your journey, whereas you pay for your taxi ride at the end. In 1986, the new shekel was introduced. These days, the shekel is a hard currency that's steadily gaining in value against other world currencies. Anyone visiting Israel on a regular basis would be wise to exchange a substantial sum of money into shekels before they return home each time: on your next visit, they will cost more to buy.

Shikker, to be shikkered

Having a drink; to be drunk.

Shuk

Market. The best known *shuk* in Tel Aviv is the Carmel Market, where in addition to food, other goods such as clothing are sold. Other worthwhile markets include the Shuk Lewinsky (for spices, nuts and tea) and the Shuk HaNamal ('Port Market'), a covered farmers' market in the old harbour.

The southern part of the city of Jaffa is best known for its Shuk HaPishpeshim ('flea market').

Shul

Yiddish word for synagogue.

Siniya

A Palestinian casserole completely covered in a layer of tahini. The casserole dish is also called a *siniya*.

Telma

Israeli food manufacturer (part of Unilever Israel).

Torah

The five books of Moses: Genesis, Exodus, Leviticus, Numbers and Deuteronomy. These first five books of the Bible are part of the Old Testament, but also have a special standing within the Jewish faith. Because of this special status, the text is hand-written on rolls of parchment using a goose-feather quill; these scrolls are sewn together, then rolled around wooden sticks. The Torah scrolls play a central role in synagogue.

Treif

Non-kosher.

Yatten

Yiddish word (also used in Dutch as 'jatten') for both 'hands' and 'to steal'.

Yeshiva

Talmud high school. Educational institute where men can study the Talmud and other Jewish religious texts.

Yodh

'Yodh' is the tenth letter of the Hebrew alphabet.

TODA (THANK YOU)

I can still remember my very first Ivrit (Modern Hebrew) lesson at Maimonides, the Jewish high school in Amsterdam. It was August 1986. To break the ice, the teacher (whose name now escapes me) asked us which Ivrit words we already knew. The girl with whom I would eventually fall in love raised her finger. 'Shalom?' The teacher nodded in agreement and wrote it in Hebrew letters on the blackboard. 'Abba,' said Naäma. 'Imma,' added the other Jigal. 'Toda,' suggested Doedoe. I knew from my holidays in Israel that this meant 'thank you'. My parents had also taught me how to say 'please', so I eagerly raised my hand, but didn't even wait to be asked. 'Bevakasha!' I cried proudly. The chalk squeaked on the board.

After we'd been round the class three times, and the blackboard was full of simple words in difficult characters, the teacher turned around. He stroked his beard theatrically with his thumb and forefinger, as he cast his eyes over all of the words. Suddenly he crossed out two of the words with quick strokes. 'These aren't used in Israel!' he roared, half joking. They were *toda* and *bevakasha*.

For a long time there was no room for courtesy within hectic Israeli society. I used to be able to set my watch by the first argument I had with some rude Israeli, which was always within five minutes of landing at Ben Gurion Airport. In stores, it was cause for celebration if you were even served. In restaurants, staff virtually threw the food on the table. Many of my classmates who pursued their dream of emigrating to Israel returned disillusioned, unable to adjust to the Israeli mentality. There's a reason why native Israeli Jews are called *sabras* (prickly pears). Like the cactus fruit, they're objectionably spiky on the outside, but nice and soft on the inside.

Increased prosperity and relative peace have buffed the rough edges from Israeli manners. Even in Jerusalem, people now rarely manage to offend like they used to. In Tel Aviv, people are cordial to one another – they're not dutiful or fawning about it, as with overly polite Americans, but sincere and jovial. *Toda* and *bevakasha* have become everyday words. Things can change. Nowadays, I'm more likely to be struck by the rudeness of the Dutch when I land at Schiphol Airport on my way home from Tel Aviv.

Toda to all the inspiring chefs who allowed me a glimpse into their kitchens: Eyal Shani, Barak Yehezkeli, Eli Shtein, Dan Zoaretz, Asaf Doktor, Jonathan Borowitz, Yuval Leshem and Ana Desai.

Toda to everyone at Nijgh & van Ditmar – especially Elik Lettinga, who called me over two years ago with an offer that I couldn't refuse. *Toda* for your patience and confidence in the successful outcome of this mega-project.

Toda to Yvette van Boven, for checking the baking recipes, to Frank Kromer and Ariëla Legman, for their critical proofreading, and to Rick Vermeer from HANOS Amsterdam, for lending us the beautiful crockery.

Toda to everyone who lent us props for the food photography, including cupboard doors, crates, boards, shutters, tabletops and newspapers: Marlyn Coetsier, Sanne Terweij, Ariel Legman, Debby Reinold, Nadia Zerouali, Esther Erwteman, Jasha van der Wel, Mark de Krom, Sheila Gogol, my parents-in-law Fred and Wil Kok and the residents of Waalstraat 93 (the bench in front of your house that we fetishised for a whole day is on page 246).

Toda to those who helped with test cooking: Marlyn Coetsier, Yael Haller, Joris Hanck, Noa Daniëlla, Merel Veel, Yvette Wurms, Mirjam Van Emden, Roos Hanck, Winnie Urban, Sandra Bolten, Marieke Spee and Stijn Bonder.

Toda to Jalon Salomon and Niels Muñoz for sharing many cosy tasting dinners – and to Shlomo

Albek for getting through the mountains of food from the photoshoots, food that would otherwise have gone to waste.

TODA to all those inspired suppliers of the best produce: Luuk and Chris from Butchery Marcus, pitta bakers Fakhar and Rachid from Maoz, Chiel from Mouwes Delicatessen, Peter and Olle from De Wijnwinkel, Mattijs from Enoteca Sprezzatura, greengrocer Ruud from Bij Ruud, Klaas from Vishandel Albert Cuyp, Jeroen from Fromagerie L'Amuse, Marian, Jan and Rado from Organic Food for You, and Daniel and Tim from Kookwinkel Duikelman.

TODA to my culinary colleagues for your inspiration and support: Jonah Freud, Yvette van Boven, Lizet Kruyff, Janny van der Heijden, Nadia Zerouali, Janneke Vreugdenhil, Joris Bijdendijk, Claudia Roden, Yotam Ottolenghi, Sylvia Witteman, Janna Gur, Ronald Giphart, Karin and Harold Hamersma, Peter Klosse, Joke Boon, Esmee Langereis, Cathy Moerdijk and Cuno van t Hoff.

TODA to my brother, Doron: without your brilliant tips I would never have discovered half the restaurants in Tel Aviv.

TODA to my dear Nienke, for being my primary proofreader, advisor, guinea pig, supporter and critic – and, of course, for your delicious challah recipe.

TODA to dear Meijer and Ada: I could not have wished for nicer children. Hopefully there will come a time when you'll actually enjoy all the (vegetable) dishes in this book.

TODA to my dear mum and dad, for your unconditional support and love, and for our wonderful home in our beloved second city. Dad: hopefully there will come a time when you'll actually enjoy all the (vegetable) dishes in this book.

Finally, a massive thank you to Team TLV, the nicest group of people I have ever worked with. Baukje, you've managed to magic a beautiful, coherent cookbook from a mountain of photos, 58,000 words and probably just as many mad ideas. Vincent, your photos are gorgeous – the hundreds of hours we spent together in Amsterdam and Tel Aviv never felt like work. Petra, where would I be without you? You were my editor-in-chief, proofreader, hand model (pages 238, 266), stylist, sous-chef, dishwasher, source of information and travelling companion – but above all the ideal mentor for this crazy project. Lovely Team TLV: TODA RABA!

Smith Street Books

Original title *TLV. Recepten en verhalen uit Tel Aviv*
First published in 2018 by Nijgh Cuisine, Amsterdam

This edition published in 2019 by Smith Street Books
Melbourne | Australia | smithstreetbooks.com

ISBN: 978-1-92581-123-0

Text & recipes © Jigal Krant
Photography © Vincent van den Hoogen* (except where
noted below)

* Jigal Krant: page 16 bottom left; page 21 bottom right; pages
  30, 41, 117, 122 bottom left; page 129 top left; pages 193, 230
  bottom right; pages 258, 265, 271 top left; pages 276, 301, 302,
  303. Petra de Hamer: page 69 bottom left and bottom right;
  page 129 top right and bottom left; page 139 top; pages 216, 217,
  271 top right, bottom left and right left. Michael Ballak: page
  257. Nienke Kok: page 230 top right.

Internal design: Wunderwald | Baukje Stamm
Cover design: Evi O, Evi O Studio
Project manager & editor-in-chief: Petra de Hamer
Culinary proofreading: Ingrid van Koppenhagen
Translation and recipe editing (English edition): Nicky Evans

Printed & bound in China by C&C Offset Printing Co., Ltd.

Book 101
10 9 8 7 6 5 4 3 2 1

תל אביב